D0216347

WITHDRAWN

HOLLYWOOD
in transition

HOLLYWOOD
in transition

RICHARD DYER MacCANN

LIBRARY
BRYAN COLLEGE
DAYTON, TENN. 37321

GREENWOOD PRESS, PUBLISHERS
WESTPORT, CONNECTICUT

79480

Library of Congress Cataloging in Publication Data

MacCann, Richard Dyer.
  Hollywood in transition.

  Reprint of the ed. published by Houghton Mifflin,
Boston.
  1. Moving-pictures--United States. I. Title.
[PN1993.5.U6M2 1977]   791.43'0973   77-5314
ISBN 0-8371-9616-7

Portions of this book have appeared in
The Christian Science Monitor and are reprinted
by permission of the copyright owner. Copyright ©
1952, 1953, 1954, 1955, 1956, 1957, 1958, 1959 by
The Christian Science Publishing Society. Chapter
4 was first published in *Film Quarterly*, Vol. XV:
No. 4. Copyright © 1962 by The Regents of the
University of California. It is reprinted by permission
of The Regents. Chapter 5 has appeared, in a
somewhat different form, in *The Yale Review*
Copyright 1962 by Yale University Press.

COPYRIGHT © 1962 BY RICHARD DYER MACCANN
ALL RIGHTS RESERVED INCLUDING THE RIGHT TO
REPRODUCE THIS BOOK OR PARTS THEREOF IN ANY FORM

Originally published in 1962 by Houghton Mifflin Company,
Boston

Reprinted with the permission of Houghton Mifflin Company

Reprinted in 1977 by Greenwood Press, Inc.

Library of Congress catalog card number 77-5314

ISBN 0-8371-9616-7

Printed in the United States of America

ACKNOWLEDGMENTS

THE ORIGIN of a book is usually obscure, even to the author. This one is mainly, I suppose, the outcome of that inevitable pressure which builds up when a professor keeps on collecting and rearranging bits of information. Yet part of the credit belongs to conversations I had with John Houseman four or five years ago. He wanted to do another analytical article about Hollywood (like the two he did for *Harper's* in 1950) and I was to help. We never got around to it, but I kept collecting people and ideas both in my classes at USC and in my columns for *The Christian Science Monitor*. Mr. Houseman owes us at least one book about his own wide-ranging contributions to radio, television, motion pictures, and the theater. Meanwhile, I owe him thanks for reading and commenting on this manuscript, chapter by chapter.

Kenneth Macgowan, professor emeritus of theater arts at UCLA, has also been kind enough to give me criticisms on the book as a whole, as have Geoffrey Shurlock, administrator of the Production Code, and James Powers, film reviewer for the *Hollywood Reporter*. Others who have read the main chapters are Arthur Knight, Arthur Mayer, King Vidor, Max Youngstein, Tom Pryor, and Lou Greenspan. Robert Vogel, Kenneth Clark, and George Stevens, Jr., helped me particularly with the chapter on the international market. None of these people, needless to say, are responsible for the way things turned out.

Special appreciation is due to Erwin Canham and *The Christian Science Monitor* for permitting extracts from the columns to be reprinted, to Dr. Tracy Strevey and the University of Southern California for a faculty grant which assisted in secretarial and research costs, to Tim Hill for guiding the book through the publication process, and to my wife for her patience with my labors and her discerning critical assistance every step of the way.

R.D.M.

PREFACE

F r e e d o m is seldom as agreeable as it looks, and never easy. The man under tyranny may long for freedom, but when he gets it he must then choose whether to establish controls of his own. If he does not set up self-controls, he incurs the loathing of others, because they are subject to the tyranny of his freedom. If he does establish, through a sense of responsibility, a reasonable system of self-restraint in his relationships with others, he chafes under the red tape of his own decisions.

The film maker, like other businessmen, always thinks he wants his own way. He cannot have it in a dictatorial state — where one man or one party may exercise erratic controls — but he cannot have it in a free market either. In a free society, the moviemaker is surrounded by the conflicting wills and needs and opinions of others. If he tries to escape from freedom (to use Erich Fromm's phrase), the easiest way is to avoid all difficult subjects and retreat to stories that are lightweight or meaningless.

If he wishes to face up to the obligations of freedom, he must be extraordinarily alert to his society's needs, ready to adjust to shifts in values, yet willing to play a role, once in a while, of leadership.

Self-restraint in Hollywood has always meant simply the Code, enforced by the major companies, the theaters, and the American public. The Code is a shadow of its former self. The major companies are now largely fragmented into independent units. They are no longer tied to theaters. The world public has become more important than the American public. These developments, step by step, have freed Hollywood of the old patterns of self-restraint.

It is the purpose of this book to describe in some detail the causes, the meaning, and the implications for the future of the four major changes that have come in the wake of the TV revolution. Those four changes are actually four expanded freedoms — freedom from censorship, freedom from centralized studio production, freedom from domination by the domestic box office, and freedom from the tyranny of the assembly line. Yet none of these freedoms, except possibly the last one, is a clear-cut advantage either for Hollywood or for society. Each new freedom carries with it new labors and new dangers, calling for courage, understanding, and a sense of obligation. If thoughtful people — in Hollywood and outside — can take a long, hard look at what has really happened, this alone will be a big step toward a better relationship between Hollywood and its new, wider world.

The combination of all four freedoms appears to have brought the individual Hollywood film producer to a new and influential status. The producer's function dates from the complex problems that came with the introduction of sound. The necessity for such a function is still not unanimously accepted in Hollywood (especially by directors), and the producer's role is difficult to define. There is no general agreement about it, even among the nearly two hundred members of the Screen Producers Guild. But in practice (and as a general rule) it is the producer who makes the major choices.

Story departments still exist in Hollywood studios, and they share with agents, stars, bankers, executives, directors, and writers many decisions along the way. But it is up to the producer (who is sometimes a producer-director or actor-producer) to decide whether he wants to make the story into a film. After that he is usually the one who picks the writer, the director, and the stars, and supervises the final editing, sound recording, and other completion chores. He may have varying degrees of power and independence. He will, if he is wise, turn over most of the artistic decisions to the director, who in turn will listen (if he is wise) to the ideas of the writer and the editor. But the producer is the man who has the responsibility for the picture.

This book is therefore concerned primarily with the producer's problems. It is also concerned with all those others who participate in the producer's problems and have power — even for a moment, in passing — to decide.

ᴛʜᴇ book is concerned primarily with the theatrical film. Another volume could be written about the fast-changing world of television since 1951. There is no question that Hollywood has become a divided town. TV film making uses up at least five or six times as much release footage per week as does theatrical film making. For some companies, TV films may make the difference between loss and profit. The TV series are the only source of steady employment for many technicians in Hollywood. Individual episodes are sometimes surprisingly good. But for the most part, TV films are thought of as the slum side of town. Every TV writer or director with any artistic inclinations longs to escape from its deadlines, its cheapness, its sameness, its mass production of crude crime and tired comedy. The feature film occupies a new position now that the "B" and "C" pictures are being made for television. That new position is the focus of analysis here.

Two familiar proverbs should perhaps be examined before the main argument begins. These two proverbs are the beginning — and often, unfortunately, the end — of most Hollywood conversations. "This," it is said, "is an entertainment business. If you have a message, send it by Western Union." Furthermore, "the reason we're in this business is not to educate or uplift people. We're in it to make money."

There is nothing wrong with these propositions as far as they go, but they don't go far enough in describing the actual world. No responsible critic of Hollywood thinks that "problem pictures" represent the chief end of movie making. Nobody wants to give up *Lili* or *Gigi* or Hitchcock. Entertainment is a vital part of any civilization. And any drama which exists solely because it started off as a lesson or preachment is almost always doomed to undramatic dullness, on the one hand, or to the irrelevant shock tactics of the western formula on the other.

The point beyond this, however, is that entertainment inevitably has an effect quite apart from its producers' intentions. The impact of any dramatic experience always carries important new information with it. Motion pictures — one at a time, and as a mounting series of visual experiences — naturally build up a cumulative educational effect. The total cultural content of the movies is what matters. And it is increasingly true that the total content of the mass communication system of a nation is an enormous factor in the cultural consciousness of all its people — even those who don't watch and listen. Every man who has the power to make a major contribution to the content of communication is a teacher and a pastor and a leader of contemporary thought and feeling, whether he rejects that role or not.

Moreover, the producer who says he's only in it for the money usually is just fooling himself — trying to put a more respectable label on an extraordinary way of life, a labor of love. When the creative producer quotes the dollar proverb, he is not necessarily speaking for himself. He means that he can't keep on making films unless he makes money for somebody else

— bankers or investors or managers of investment funds.

But the characteristic tension of show business seems to foster outlandish expectations. There is always a chance of spectacular losses; therefore every single film must hold forth a promise of spectacular gains. Making money isn't enough. A comfortable return on the over-all investment isn't enough. Every film must make a lot of money — a big pile of money — before it can be called a success and really satisfy the investors. Such an exaggeration of the right to make money eventually does damage to the free enterprise system. The urge to make a killing is not the same thing as the right to a fair return, and it poisons the movie business perhaps more than any other.

As for those producers and executives who claim to have accepted the dollar proverb as their own working rationale, one or two direct questions may be in order. In the final analysis, what is the money for? After wearing out the pleasures of ostentation, travel, and purchased companionship, what then? A collection of paintings and sculpture? Why not contribute instead to the art of the film?

Perhaps a man will claim he wants money in order to provide the finest advantages for his children. Why not also provide them with a better world? The world those privileged young people will live in is not going to be very much improved just because certain men made a pile of money — and gave some of it to charity. But there is always a good chance that their world might be touched and enriched by the art of the film.

CONTENTS

PREFACE   vii

Part I. Hollywood's Four Freedoms

1. HURRY AND WAIT   3

2. THE BIG SHIFT   10

3. FROM TECHNOLOGY TO ADULTERY   20
   Stretching the Screen   21
   The Pleasures of Maturity   27
   Lessons in Delinquency   33
   Adultery for the Whole Family?   42

4. INDEPENDENCE WITH A VENGEANCE   50
   Agents and Actors Become Producers   50
   The Cautious Independent Chooses Terror   59
   A Touch of Paternalism in a No Man's Land?   65

5. HOLLYWOOD FACES THE WORLD   71
   The Competitive Foreign Market   72
   Pressures for Overseas Production   79
   Pleasing Everybody in the World   83

The Melodramatic Image of America   87
Restriction or Responsibility?   93

6. THE END OF THE ASSEMBLY LINE   104
    The Overproduced Picture   104
    The Gray Flannel Men and the Decline of Style   110

7. CAN HOLLYWOOD HELP ITSELF?   116
    Four Freedoms — and Three Limitations   116
    Don't Look Back!   121
    The Closed Front Door   125
    Secondhand Seeing   132

Part II. Hollywood at Work

INTRODUCTION   145

1. PRODUCERS   149
    The Independence of David O. Selznick   149
    Sam Spiegel on the River Kwai   151
    Ross Hunter: Glamour First   154
    Samuel Goldwyn on Leadership and Excitement   157

2. DIRECTORS   161
    Delmer Daves' Route to the Top   161
    Elia Kazan and the Veneer of Civilization   163
    The Notebooks of George Stevens   167
    William Wyler on Peace and Realism   170

3. WRITERS   173
    Dissent by Dudley Nichols   173
    Frank Gruber's Seven Basic Western Plots   175
    Cary Grant Is Dissatisfied with Writers   177

4. STARS   181
    Janet Leigh's Zest for Living   181
    William Holden, World Traveler   183
    Marlon Brando on Achieving Understanding   185
    James Dean and the High School Kids   187
    Joanne Woodward Works from the Outside In   189
    Judy Holliday Analyzes Comedy   192
    Alec Guinness Wins His First Laugh   195

5. THE CHANGING SCENE   198
    Raymond Hatton Remembers the Silent Days   198
    Hannibal's Elephants in Southern California   200
    TV Tools for Hollywood?   203
    The Vanishing Back Lot   206

PART I

Hollywood's Four Freedoms

1

HURRY AND WAIT

"The ambition of a Latin-American revolutionary;
the ego of a grand opera tenor; and the physical
stamina of a cow pony."

Billie Burke on the qualifications
for survival in Hollywood

THE MOST familiar, solid, bedrock certainty in Hollywood is sudden change. It is one of the least understood facts about the Hollywood scene. Its influence permeates every aspect of life in the movie capital. It is partly a result of the temperamental personalities naturally attracted to show business as a career. It is a reflection of the impulsive shifts of public taste and attention. But it is also inherent in the way pictures are made.

A new picture, when it starts, means an intensive new experience for a group of from fifty to one hundred people. There is a long period of preparation beforehand, to be sure. The decision to buy a story may mean the setting up of a completely new independent corporation. The producer has to choose his point of view, work it out in collaboration with the screenwriter, prepare sets and costumes, select the director, cast, and crew. He has to decide whether to shoot the picture in Hollywood or "on location" — perhaps thousands of miles away.

But suddenly, on the day shooting begins, there they
are — all together — the tight little group of people who
are going to make the picture. They must constantly in-
teract with each other emotionally, in front of the camera
or behind it.

The day's work is scheduled in a general way. Actually it is an unpredictable round of hurry-and-wait. Intense, brief scenes before the camera and microphone are
followed by long delays for new setups. A day's work
may cover no more than two or three minutes of screen
time. For most of the crew, the day lasts from eight in
the morning till six at night.

Then, after a few weeks, the shooting is over. The producer, editor, musicians, and publicity men are still working hard. But the cast and crew are through. Until the
next job begins, they literally have time on their hands,
all day every day. Having been intensely busy, they are
now totally relaxed. For some of them, especially the actors, such relaxation is impossible. They go to Palm
Springs, the races, the movies, New York, Europe, the
nearest little theater group, the nearest bar.

This enormous contrast between feverish activity and
sudden letdown has become more pronounced than ever
before. Theatrical movie making has gradually become
different from any other way of life in the history of show
business. Its stresses and strains are even more insistent
than in the theater. A stage production at least may develop into a long-run hit, offering some security and activity for a year or more. A movie, however, is made only

once. In the old days of silent films, there were so many pictures made that nearly everybody was under contract from year to year and actually made pictures one after the other in dizzy, happy succession. With the advent of sound, skyrocketing costs, and higher standards for stories, the old assembly-line system has slowed to a walk.

Today, contracts are rare and pictures are few. The typical top director, actor, writer, or producer may have a contract with a releasing company for only one or two pictures a year — with options to do one film outside or to work in television. The typical crew member has to wait for a call from the union to join one of these once-a-year projects when it is ready to go. Hurry-and-wait, so typical of the production process on the set, has become a way of life. And the waiting periods — except for a handful of stars and directors in "top demand" at the moment — grow longer and longer.

The effect on patterns of employment is obvious. In the old days, when a man was on a steady studio contract, the studio had to keep finding a job for him, so that he would be busy and productive while being paid. Today he has to look for work by himself — that is, he has to have an agent look for it for him — from month to month and year to year. Long before he begins a new job he must start searching for the one to come after it. He achieves no comfortable seniority or bureaucratic respectability — only a "reputation," fanned by publicity about the latest picture he has worked on. He puts himself on sale every day of his life.

For some, the arrival of television has made things easier, or at least more interesting. Actors and writers can keep busy, every once in a while, with filmed short stories or ninety-minute dramatic "specials" if they can schedule them between pictures. Some actors and many directors and technicians have had to make the decision to go all the way over and work on a TV series. TV film making means they are in another world altogether. They have no time for anything or anybody until those thirty-nine pictures are shot and in the can. Then the hiatus comes and they're back on the block once more, looking for work. They can rest for a while on their residuals, to be sure. But residual payments are neither dependable nor eternal. And the longer an actor or director stays out of circulation the less likely he is to be "remembered" for another job.

Security is almost unknown in Hollywood. It is a dream, a fantastic concept remembered from some fairy tale about life outside. And because it is a dream, it is constantly sought.

The appearance of security may be sought by investing in sleek cars and lavish homes. This is a familiar twentieth century concern in most American communities. Models change. Neighborhoods become less fashionable. It is necessary to possess the latest Cadillac and make occasional moves in order to keep others aware of one's status. In Hollywood there is little security in this, after all, because acceptance — even social acceptance — is largely dependent on the next picture.

Few Hollywood people can afford to take the time for extensive contacts outside of the industry. The ever present necessity is to use social events to reinforce job seeking, consciously or subconsciously. This lack of contact with the real world makes it harder to find acceptance among the Hollywood community for stories about the common life of ordinary Americans.

At the story-buying level, there is a similar longing for "properties" which will be "sure-fire." In the past, the search was for formulas — the repeated plot patterns a supposedly static public mind would accept. Today this is left to television, and the search is for established, "presold" novels or plays. At a lower budgetary level, smaller producers may also try to move in early on some developing "cycle" of subjects.

Everybody knows that every long-run stage show can't hit the screen like *Oklahoma!* Every novel can't be expected to become a phenomenon on film like *Gone With the Wind.* Rare is the cycle, too, that holds at the box office for very long. But man's need for certainty is more insistent than logic. When a Broadway stage success or a best-selling novel is purchased, everyone remotely connected with the project agrees that the film version is bound to be a great success. Everybody goes along with the dream.

The search for security is not peculiar to the movie business, of course. The big difference is that the movie business is concerned with the public's search for something quite different: excitement and adventure.

Here, then, is another reason for the constancy of change in Hollywood. Film distributors call it the fickleness of the public. It is, more accurately, the natural desire of the public to find something new to enjoy, something that takes them out of their daily routine, on the one hand, or something that adds to their knowledge of life and their zest of living, on the other. If the escape itself becomes routine, the public will turn away from that, too. Inevitably the public's search for adventure becomes more unpredictable all the time, as life itself becomes more complex and the public better informed about life through other media of communication.

The human personality, psychologists say, needs both familiarity and adventure, both security and change. The star may represent familiarity. This is a kind of security for producer and public alike. But the advertising must also insist: "Never before such danger! Never before such passion!" Some part of the total experience inside the movie house must be new, different, memorable, worthy of being "talked about."

This is the basic problem of the film producer. He must serve a constantly changing taste with a constantly different product. The movie audience is not buying steel or a supply of lumber or a refrigerator. Movies are not necessary for modern life in statistically predictable amounts. Nor can they be reproduced over and over again even within the yearly limits of changes in fashion, like automobiles or women's dresses. Every single item manufactured has to be different. Every single item has to be separately sold, and sold on the basis that the purchaser goes away with nothing tangible whatever — nothing more than an imaginary adventure, an emotional experience.

The theatrical film producer is forced to respond to some image he has of a probable audience. The director, writer, actors, and technicians can only respond to the producer's guesses. The work they all do is erratic in its timing, emotional by its nature, and always temporary. Change is the essence of daily life in Hollywood. If this is not understood, nothing else about Hollywood can be satisfactorily explained.

2

THE BIG SHIFT

"Don't be a 'Living Room Captive.' Step out and
see a great movie!"

Industry advertisement, 1952

THE ACCEPTANCE of television is too big a change,
and in many ways too well known, to try to tell in full.
But because the upsurge of TV has set the very channels
of change in other respects — and for the future — some
of its outlines will be set down here.

In the fall of 1951, the microwave relay was completed
across the American continent — in time for the Japanese
treaty conference and the world series. After that, the
battle was fully joined between the networks and the film
makers.

At first it seemed there might be only two kinds of
reaction in Hollywood. One favorite line of thought insisted on taking TV lightly. According to this view, movies still belonged in theaters. The living room fad would
pass. Most people eventually would find that they still
preferred to go out and mingle with other people. They
would look for their "best" entertainment on a big
screen, without interruptions by commercials, telephone

calls, or youngsters bawling from the bedroom.

The other kind of reaction, especially on the production and distribution front, was to fight TV with every weapon at hand. No contract actors should be permitted to appear on network shows. No old films should be sold to the electronic monster. Even buying TV advertising for movies was looked on with suspicion. The notion of making newfangled half-hour films on the major lots was inconceivable. All the theatergoing public really desired was better films. And of course the veteran artists of the Hollywood studios would go right on making them.

As everyone knows, these dreamlike defenses soon broke down, at least in part. It is now clear that most people above the age of twenty or twenty-five would much rather stay home after a hard day. They are glad to have their entertainment handed to them on a commercial platter in the privacy of their living rooms.

The theater audience has been cut at least in half. Large claims of an average ninety million customers a week in the early postwar years have now been reduced to claims of a weekly forty or forty-five million today, with something like the old peak audience returning in a few weeks of summertime, when young people are on vacation.

The total number of theaters has not shown a comparatively dizzy decline, because of the rise of "drive-in's." But "hard top" theaters are increasingly hard pressed. For every new drive-in constructed in the last ten years, a regular theater, with seats, has gone to the wall. The relative status of drive-ins has now reached a fairly stable point. Further stabilization is resulting in an absolute decline in the numbers of theaters.

No one could have foreseen such a fast-moving shift. Theaters, ten years ago, were thought by many investors to be a more profitable side of the entertainment business than production companies. Now it is clear that every theater must survive on the merits of the "product" it shows and the showmanship that sells it. Theatrical exhibition is no longer the primary way of reaching the public with motion pictures.

This was made painfully clear when old Hollywood movies started showing up on TV in large numbers. Short-term economic pressures forced the movie companies to sell thousands of old features to TV. Big lump sums were added to company ledgers by those sales. But large segments of the remaining theater audience vanished into the living rooms at the same time. There, it seemed, old movies were the best entertainment. It was a great opportunity to study film history, but theater men were hardly interested in that aspect of the situation. They were not surprised by a report of the Sindlinger organization which chronicled a drastic drop in theater attendance at the time the bulk of the feature films were released on TV.

Battling television on the production front didn't last long, either. As policy or as practice, it gradually became untenable. Increasingly among the voices of resistance were those who said, in a new tone of voice altogether:

"They'll have to come to us in the long run! Eventually the veterans of the Hollywood major studios will make the pictures for television too."

As early as 1951, a major studio was in production. Columbia Pictures set up a subsidiary called Screen Gems, which undertook to provide half-hour films on the new three-day TV production schedules under the studio roof. MCA, one of the top three talent agencies, decided there was gold in the kilocycle hills if it could only be "packaged." Offering its own agency list of writers, directors, and stars, neatly put together in various comedy, melodrama, or "anthology" series, MCA found the advertising agencies more than willing to talk business with its new subsidiary, Revue Productions.

It was a slow adjustment, and it did not involve, after all, amalgamations of networks and studios. Small film companies arose on every side. Some made specific series for network use. Others explored the trickier process of sale by syndication to stations around the country. One of the early organizations was a little company known as Desilu, producer of a new comedy series called "I Love Lucy."

Tiny companies all over town also began to get contracts from the agencies for producing commercial "spot" messages to tie in with TV shows. Animation studios, especially, discovered that commercials could be their bread-and-butter accounts, and a whole new tradition of humor in advertising began.

The big breakthrough by a major studio was Walt Disney's decision to diversify. "Disneyland" began in October, 1954. It was not only an exceptionally good TV show, for children and for their families. It was also a colossal business parlay, with an air of impudence about it that more than ever forced Hollywood to admire the inimitable Walt and his "business brother," Roy.

The Disney TV show opened ahead of the now famous carnival showplace in Anaheim. One of its main functions was to act as a year-long preview advertisement for that wonderful playground. In addition, it was an advertisement for all of the Disney theatrical features — new ones and reissues. Frequently the whole hour was spent simply "plugging" a forthcoming film. The TV screen revealed secrets of production behind the scenes and clips from the picture itself.

All of this was paid for, eagerly and cheerfully, by other people — by manufacturers of products for sale in grocery stores, drugstores, and automobile showrooms. The product advertiser paid the network for the time and paid the Disney studio for his production cost (plus a profit), and then paid the advertising agency for granting him the privilege of paying Disney and the networks. After that, the same advertisers (plus some others) gladly paid Mr. Disney for the additional privilege of buying small plots of exclusive real estate in his new kingdom in Anaheim.

Naturally the other film companies were fascinated. It was like playing leapfrog. Everybody helped everybody else. The consumer, of course, paid the bill. It was especially gratifying to receive money from someone else for advertising your films, instead of paying for the advertising in the generally accepted manner.

The next year Warner Brothers and Twentieth Century–Fox, with varying results, tried to do exactly what Disney had done. Their hour-long dramatic stories were interspersed with behind-scenes commercials for forthcoming films. It was not the same. Disney had blithely spent a whole show on his previews of coming attractions, and somehow the result was delightful. Fox and Warners only managed to make it sound like double commercials. Nor did the scripts (taken from the backlog in their story departments) have the variety and distinction of Disney's, which ranged from fairy-tale to nonfiction in Fantasyland, Tomorrowland, Frontierland, and Adventureland.

But the precedent was laid down. The break was made. The majors were deeply involved in TV film production.

M-G-M fumbled its early attempts to do weekly shows. Not till "The Thin Man" did the most famous studio of them all come around to a somewhat successful format for a TV series. And one day in the daily trades there appeared an advertisement which shocked many an old hand in Hollywood. It announced that Metro-Goldwyn-Mayer was in the business of producing filmed commercials. The biggest movie lot in Los Angeles was so inactive that its owners were soliciting the smallest form of television production. Surely this sounded like the end of the "battle." Perhaps even the end of the transition was in sight.

It was Lucille Ball and her then husband Desi Arnaz who most of all symbolized the newness of the era. After five years of extraordinary popularity as a TV comedy team, they not only owned or helped to produce as many as a dozen other shows but they had enough credit to buy a major motion picture lot. The old RKO-Radio studio and its Culver City counterpart, RKO-Pathé, were renamed the Desilu Studios.

Meanwhile, any attempts to keep contract stars off TV had ended with the contracts. Employment arrangements began to change anyway, by mutual agreement. Television's competition was forcing a whole new pattern of fewer and costlier pictures, which meant the studios could no longer afford long-term exclusive contracts. Many film actors were eager for the excitement of working in a series on TV, or at least more often than twice a year. They turned up more and more frequently on anthology dramas. Some of them were even willing to learn the many lines required for "live" performances.

In general, it has been discovered that entertainment traffic can move both ways quite successfully. Movie stories have been made the basis for TV series. TV scripts have become movies. Actors have gained fame in one medium and moved into the other. A few producers and directors have found it possible to work in both. Technicians, too, have moved freely back and forth in the two kinds of film making, although many who grew up in the easygoing days of motion picture production have found it impossible to adjust to a three-day film-making schedule.

Is the transition over? An uneasy state of mutual acceptance seems to prevail. Certainly it is no longer possible to ignore TV or to fight it on any basis but artistic competition. The old attitudes look foolish in the light of recent history.

For the last two or three years, according to Richard W. Jencks, president of the Alliance of Television Film Producers, about three thousand TV films, adding up to more than one hundred different series, were made annually in Hollywood. Nearly three fourths of the forty thousand people employed in motion pictures in the Hollywood area owe their work directly or indirectly to TV film activity.

The argument that "they will have to come to us" has proved to be only partly true. In 1962, only twenty-six series could be attributed to the "old" major companies. Warner Brothers and Columbia are the only ones that can be said to have achieved successful diversification. M-G-M is beginning to get the hang of it, but Twentieth Century–Fox is trailing in the race, while Paramount (by early 1962) still hadn't sold a series, and Universal wasn't trying. Disney, of course, has limited himself to his own show. United Artists has bought into Ziv, a veteran syndication company.

The apparent purpose of all this activity — and the new

ways of life worked out by a new breed of studio TV producers with advertising agency men — is to pay for basic studio overhead. Television production keeps some of the sound stages occupied and some of the key studio departments staffed. But the big profits — and the big gambles — are still the big pictures. A major studio, like a major automobile manufacturer, can't survive on narrow-margin items alone. The right combination of compacts and Cadillacs can keep the Hollywood system going for quite a while, especially if there are also some real estate profits, a few oil wells, and a batch of best-selling popular records to put into the annual stockholders' report.

Perhaps the major development in the rapidly diversifying Hollywood scene is the rise of the "new majors" in TV film-making. Revue Productions, recently forced by the Screen Actors Guild to split off from its parent talent agency, MCA, makes more filmed series than any other company in town. Desi Arnaz rents the stages on his three lots to a variety of independent TV companies, some of them owned in part by his Desilu company. Four Star's actor-president, Dick Powell, also decided some time ago that his corporation needed regular access to sound stages: he has leased Republic studio, which echoed for many years to the shouts and gunshots of bottom-drawer feature-length westerns.

The main reason for the success of these new companies is their ability to shift into the high gear required by television — three days for a half-hour show, five or six days for an hour show. Nevertheless, each of these three companies now has plans to undertake, from time to time, the big gamble for the big profits of feature film production.

Pay-Television looms on the Hollywood horizon like a glorious, sure-fire gold rush. The chance for colossal box-office returns in a single night is a stake for which nearly every film producer in town would gladly offer up his shirt. Some day that beckoning bonanza (with its wonderful prospect of bypassing the costs of prints and distribution to theaters) may reach solid actuality on studio production schedules. When it does, veteran feature film makers may hope to elbow aside the "three-day wonders" of the new TV assembly lines. But they may also discover that the little fellows have already diversified upward, and are prepared to make feature films faster than anybody. When that happens, the historic battle against TV as a medium of distribution will be only a memory.

3

FROM TECHNOLOGY TO ADULTERY

"Why not keep the theater screens the same size
and simply reduce the size of the audience?"

Irving Breecher, quoted in
Daily Variety, *April 1953*

THE COMPLETION of the transcontinental microwave relay was not the only signal for upheaval in Hollywood. Something else happened in the show-business
world which was both a threat and a promise.

The opening of *This Is Cinerama* in New York on September 20, 1952, was one of the great events in motion
picture history. It had some of the same excitement as
Edison's first projection of motion pictures on a screen in
Koster and Bial's music hall in 1896.

The critics were swept off their feet. Archer Winsten
of the New York *Post* said that "it creates illusions of
movement and live sound that are incomparably more
powerful than anything yet viewed on the screen." Bosley Crowther observed in the New York *Times* that "people sat back in spellbound wonder as the scenic program
flowed across the screen. It was really as though most of
them were seeing motion pictures for the first time."

This Is Cinerama was among the top ten attractions in

the country for more than a year. Five years later, operating in only twenty cities in the United States — and eight cities in foreign countries — the first Cinerama show had grossed more than $25,000,000.

Here was an "attraction" taking in dollars that might have gone to regular movies. But it was also pulling people out of their homes, away from their TV sets. It was a sign and a portent. Film executives immediately wondered if technological change was the answer to their problem of the vanishing audience. They remembered that the arrival of sound had been a lifesaver for Warner Brothers and was a factor in putting off for a while the effects of the 1929 depression. As in the case of sound, they delayed and worried and wondered what to do.

Stretching the Screen

A man from radio was the first to be heard from. For United Artists release, Arch Oboler wrote and directed independently a simple little story about game hunters in Africa called *Bwana Devil*. He actually shot most of it in the brown hills northwest of Los Angeles. He used an enormous camera that took two pictures at once, "seeing" in three dimensions like the human eyes. It was a very bad picture and it made a great deal of money.

This was another shock. Obviously the American people were fascinated by new technical gimmicks. Warner Brothers decided to make a 3-D horror picture, *House of Wax*. It was not only terrifying. It was terrible. But the public evidently loved to see things coming out of the screen at them, even if they had to wear special polaroid glasses to get the effect. Some of the first-run theaters installed amplifiers at the sides and back of the auditorium for a three-dimensional effect in sound. This scared the customers, too, and the money rolled in.

At the height of the 3-D production era in Hollywood, I had a talk with Milton Gunzburg, one of the owners of Natural Vision Corporation. His company, besides claiming certain patent rights to equipment, was distributing millions of disposable polaroid glasses to theater owners all over the country. He spoke expansively of the future, when the "realism" of the motion picture would be more startling than ever. As I bade him goodbye at the door of his Sunset Boulevard mansion, I said I would look him up in another year and see how the future had turned out.

There wasn't much point in keeping that promise. As it happened, we met at a CinemaScope preview more than a year later. There wasn't much to say. Hollywood had already forgotten him.

Why did 3-D fail? Was it because the first pictures were poor in story quality? The public never saw the 3-D version of Alfred Hitchcock's *Dial M for Murder*. Was it because everybody hated to wear glasses? Certainly the people who already wore glasses of their own were doubly annoyed. Was it because 3-D is essentially a "gimmick" which attracts attention to itself? A chandelier suddenly advancing out of the frame inevitably becomes more important than the young lovers underneath.

These factors were all of some importance. But the next big response to TV and Cinerama was the decision by Twentieth Century–Fox to adopt a wide-screen system. This was the real deathblow for 3-D. The focus of Hollywood attention shifted to CinemaScope, and the public followed that focus.

The decision took courage. It staked millions of dollars and the future of the Fox studio on an invention which had been available for many years — an optical system which condensed on a 35-millimeter frame of film a much wider field of vision. It meant that both cameras and projectors had to have new lens attachments. It meant that theaters would have to install wider screens. Theater men, already involved with special beaded screens and interlocked projectors for 3-D exhibition, protested violently. Spyros Skouras and Darryl Zanuck simply pointed to the weekly boxoffice of Cinerama. They announced they were going ahead to make every one of their films in the new "anamorphic" system.

A few months later they could also point to the staggering box-office returns from *The Robe*, their first Cinema-Scope production. They had chosen their costliest picture of the year for Hollywood's first wide-screen experiment, and it was an impressive success. This was no cautious one shot tryout with a mediocre magic show. It was an all-out bid for public favor. It was promptly followed by a comedy, *How to Marry a Millionaire*, and a series of other pictures with enough variety to satisfy the most nervous exhibitor.

Obviously CinemaScope (proportions, 2 to 5) could do almost anything the old-fashioned frame (proportions, 3 to 4) could do. Some Hollywood engineers and cameramen were sorry to give up the more elaborate challenges of 3-D photography, but the studios were relieved. A wider screen was easier to understand. It was also more of a challenge to television. Already there had been public tests of 3-D on TV. Installation of a seventy-foot screen, on the other hand, seemed a fairly remote prospect for the average American living room.

Bigness had its limitations, to be sure. If you sat in the back of the balcony, the screen looked about the same size as it did from the middle of the theater before. If you sat near the front, you were likely to come away with battered eyes and a twisted neck.

Aesthetically, the new framing process had serious drawbacks. CinemaScope was designed in part to appease the larger theater owners, who got much of their income from balcony patrons. The height of the screen had to be kept uniform with the old height so that patrons sitting under the balcony wouldn't be deprived of the upper part of the picture. The result was a "ribbon," not the steep grandeur of Cinerama. Because of the odd proportions, single close-ups became much less pleasing (unless they were "balanced" by a lamp or a doorway). Because of the larger total area, even "two shots" made the faces look big and baleful.

CinemaScope was the antithesis of the art of the film, as this phrase has been generally accepted by directors,

critics, historians, and students. Its characteristic effect
on the director was to force him to imitate the stage. This
had happened twice before in the history of the motion
picture — once when Adolph Zukor discovered that "famous players" from Broadway and overseas multiplied
his receipts from silent films, and again when the arrival
of sound demanded trained actors who could speak effectively. CinemaScope's technical "advancement" suggested stage technique for a different reason. The action
was most easily framed as if by a proscenium arch.
Larger spatial areas could be held longer on the screen
and still be made interesting — that is, if the camera or
the characters moved once in a while. This meant fewer
camera setups and a certain amount of saving in cost both
in shooting and editing.

The art of the film as developed by D. W. Griffith was
quite different from such a theatrical concept. The regular size screen had depended heavily on close shots, cutting quickly from one to another to achieve story information, emotional tone, and visual style. CinemaScope directors, cameramen, and editors had much less chance
for variety or intimacy. Now the characteristic shot was
the medium shot of two persons rather than the close-up
of one face.

Furthermore, the framing itself was widely agreed to
be unnatural from an aesthetic standpoint. George Stevens once showed me a whole series of books containing
reproductions of paintings. Some, of course, were square,
or nearly so. Some were tall and narrow, a few low and

wide. Artists are free to choose their own composition and frame accordingly. Motion picture makers had accepted the 3 x 4 frame as the best compromise for most purposes. Mr. Stevens' point was that a long, low frame was rarely "right" and certainly wrong for regular use.

"CinemaScope is fine," he shrugged, "if you want a system that shows a boa constrictor to better advantage than a man."

Later I asked Darryl Zanuck how he proposed, for example, to frame the spire of a church in CinemaScope. "Pan up with the camera," he replied confidently. He went on to praise a recent camera test for *How to Marry a Millionaire* — a panorama shot from a taxicab, tilting up to the top of a skyscraper.

CinemaScope has survived, despite its critics. Mr. Stevens himself agreed to do *The Diary of Anne Frank* in the 2 x 5 ratio, although he held out for black-and-white photography. At first, regular size films persisted in winning the Academy Award for best production, but a bigger version of the wide-screen idea won top honors in 1956 — *Around the World in 80 Days,* made in Todd-AO.

The size and shape of the screen caught the attention of the public, as Mr. Zanuck thought it would. He was also wise enough, however, to throw into the breach a large number of good stories. Some were reworked old favorites; few of them were merely remakes. For a while, the novelty held up. For a while, Hollywood could still be a factory.

The Pleasures of Maturity

As the audience began to fall away once more, most Hollywood producers were aware that the next line of defense could not be some new form of technology. Film makers now would have to be concerned with content. The story would have to be the thing.

The story had to be more "different," more exciting than ever. To some producers, this naturally meant the oldest defense of all — more sex and violence.

Here again, the first breakthrough was by a strong individual. Otto Preminger decided that *The Moon Is Blue* was the kind of talk-fest about sex which would attract a lot of customers in a Freud-conscious age. Yet it probably could be defended in terms of the Production Code. He was wrong on the last count. In the final event, the picture was denied a seal of approval and also condemned by the Roman Catholic Legion of Decency.

The producer-director determined on a broadside attack on the Code itself. Full of righteous wrath, he made the issue a *cause célèbre*, a matter of film's freedom to speak. The public supported his right of free speech, perhaps the more ardently since the speech was supposed to be naughty.

The Moon Is Blue was refused by some theater circuits which were loyal to the Code and fearful of the Legion. Its notoriety, however, made up for those losses in the theaters which carried it. Here the divorcement of theaters from production companies profited the producer—

and even some exhibitors. Since theater chains were no longer joined to production companies, they were not members of the Motion Picture Association and not bound by the Production Code. United Artists, distributor of the picture, withdrew from the MPA long enough for the film to make the rounds.

Mr. Preminger was well satisfied. He prepared to produce *The Man with the Golden Arm,* a melodrama about narcotics addiction. This was a subject specifically forbidden by the Code. He made it, got it exhibited (this time without Legion of Decency condemnation), and came out with a profit. In due time, the Code itself was revised to permit such subjects.

Hollywood did not miss the lesson. The film capital is divided three ways, as most people are, on the subject of self-censorship. Some say that restraint is all-important because the historic reputation of Hollywood movies as "family entertainment" must be upheld. A second group insists, on the other hand, that the art of the film is constantly in conflict with the barriers of puritanism and must seek to break through with stories that probe human nature more and more deeply. A third, much larger group — which actually includes many of those appearing to argue on the other two sides of the question — is concerned simply with money. For most Hollywood people, the issue is only a matter of prediction: which will bring in more money this year, "art" or self-restraint?

There were other straws in the wind. They all seemed to point to a changing subject matter for the screen.

The Tennessee Williams play, *A Streetcar Named Desire*, had been a great success as a film. So had the James Jones novel, *From Here to Eternity*. Foreign pictures were increasingly successful in the smaller "art" theaters and seemed to be successful in proportion to their advertised "frankness." A restless, prosperous public, with more leisure and more luxuries, seemed eager to toy with forbidden things.

Television, the competitive reason for developing a "new look" in the first place, seemed to be helping to make it possible. Live dramatic shows were becoming less and less daring, more and more subservient to sponsor fears of pressure-group criticism. Their scripts were beginning to be carefully pruned by "continuity departments." The pressure-group concern about TV, at the same time, was obviously going to take away some of the pressure on theatrical film makers.

To many in Hollywood it seemed clear that the movies must move toward what was called maturity — or "adult subjects." Jerry Wald, like the Cecil B. deMille of an earlier era, was quick to sense the box-office trend. "We must explore," he said, "more of the closed rooms of human experience and personality: the half-light of evil, guilt, conscience." Mr. Wald had purchased the rights to *Peyton Place*. The sensational story was thoroughly scrubbed up for the screen, but it did contain a few new words and situations. The very act of purchase was symbolic of the trend.

Evidently best-selling books and popular plays were

going to be made into pictures regardless of the traditions of the Code. Meanwhile the Code itself was generally revised and simplified in wording, so that decisive action was more than ever left to the discretion of its administrators. And the administrators, of course, including their knowledgeable and popular chief, Geoffrey Shurlock, were no more than employees of the major companies in the MPA. Their advice in detail would still be listened to with respect, but they could have little to say about the trend.

After all, the reason for having a code was to keep out of the movies anything that the handful of state censor boards might later insist on removing. These very censor boards were now in a state of rapid decline. The U.S. Supreme Court, while striking down the New York state ban on the Italian film *The Miracle,* had finally decided to include the motion picture screen among the elements of free speech guaranteed by the First Amendment to the Constitution. Film-making was no longer, by legal decree, merely an "entertainment business." Film makers (the court said in effect) should be left as free as newspaper publishers. The scope of state censorship was therefore contracted to the narrow but undecided limits of obscenity. Suddenly the powers of precensoring bodies had become relatively unimportant in those few states where they existed. The legal environment had fundamentally changed.

And so, a little at a time, a few of the biggest pictures each year began to make new assumptions about the kind of experience the audience wanted — and the kind of knowledge the audience brought to the theater.

Comedies like *The Seven Year Itch, The Tender Trap, Love in the Afternoon, Ask Any Girl,* and *Rally 'Round the Flag, Boys* followed the lead of *The Moon Is Blue.* A *Hatful of Rain* was allowed to deal with narcotics under the liberalized Code. Even *Tea and Sympathy* was adapted for the screen by avoiding outright assertions about homosexuality.

In a middle range of significance, solemn soap operas like *No Down Payment, Ten North Frederick, Too Much Too Soon, Anatomy of a Murder,* and *The Story on Page One* assumed that the public wanted to know just a little more about the "closed rooms of human experience," and the films were advertised accordingly.

In 1958, the year of *Anna Lucasta* and *God's Little Acre,* William Faulkner was also carefully adjusted to the new mood in *The Long Hot Summer* (and the following year in *The Sound and the Fury*). But Tennessee Williams became the chief symbol of the new "freedom" of the screen, and his plays provided the most controversial material, year by year: *Baby Doll* (1956), *Cat on a Hot Tin Roof* (1958), and *Suddenly Last Summer* (1959). Each of these theatricalized case studies in frustrated sex relationships stirred increasing opposition among parent and civic groups.

In 1960, Jerry Wald added D. H. Lawrence to the Hollywood list of authors with a version of *Sons and Lovers* so delicately handled it seemed little more than a family quarrel. Billy Wilder, in a story of immorality among corporation executives, made *The Apartment* a tragi-comedy infused with moral indignation. But these better-than-average achievements were surrounded by a rising tide of sex-centered stories like *Home from the Hill, Studs Lonigan,* and *Strangers When We Meet.*

Of *Butterfield 8* Dick Williams said in the Los Angeles *Mirror-News*: "The emphasis is almost entirely and unrelievedly on sex." In *From the Terrace,* according to James Powers in the *Hollywood Reporter,* "Newman has driven his wife, Joanne Woodward, to seek love elsewhere . . . Newman's solution, however, is to leave his wife, now a jaded sensualist, for another love." *Daily Variety* gave this view of *The Fugitive Kind*: "Joanne Woodward . . . pops in and out of the story to provide a ludicrous and distasteful extra dash of degeneracy. The scene in a cemetery where she attempts a carnal relation with Brando reaches a new low in suggestive animalism." In *Let No Man Write My Epitaph, Time* Magazine explains, "The hero starts life with prospects that are not, to put it mildly, brilliant . . . He is the illegitimate son of a convicted killer and B-Girl Winters, who is hooked by — and sleeping with — a dope peddler." In *The Bramble Bush,* according to Margaret Harford of the Los Angeles *Mirror-News,* "adultery and illegitimacy are simply the main problems. There are numerous minor ones like seduction, perversion, blackmail, arson, alcoholism, and insanity." *Private Property* was explained thus by

Philip K. Scheuer of the Los Angeles *Times*: "The movie details the methodical, step-by-step seduction of a sex-starved Hollywood Hills housewife by a beatnik who is preparing her for the arms of his weak-willed (and, as it develops, impotent) kooky-pal." Hollis Alpert, in the *Saturday Review,* commented: "The Production Code seal . . . has been given *The World of Suzie Wong,* a clear vote in favor of prostitution as a suitable subject for the family motion picture audience."

And in 1961, William Wyler remade *The Children's Hour,* this time with full attention to the lesbian aspects of the story, and Otto Preminger, once more breaking the Code in full confidence that his picture would not be hurt by it, produced and directed the motion picture version of *Advise and Consent,* in which a U.S. Senator is accused of homosexuality. The result, even before release of either picture, was a statement by the Motion Picture Association that the absolute ban in the Code against any subject dealing with perversion was, in effect, lifted — if dealt with in good taste.

Lessons in Delinquency

Earlier, another old trend had reached a new turning point. For years, Dore Schary had defended "the message picture" as having a legitimate place on the screens of the world. Movies, of course, should follow public opinion, not lead it, he insisted. But a good dramatic story based on a current issue could be a winner at the box office, besides stirring up the kind of discussion that is healthy in a democracy.

Mr. Schary had represented this point of view in Hollywood ever since he produced *Crossfire,* at RKO, based on a novel by Richard Brooks called *The Brick Foxhole.* In its film version, it was an attack on anti-Semitism, and the plot was developed with the usual elements of close physical conflict so familiar in the westerns and the gangster films.

By now, Mr. Schary was established as chief of production at Metro-Goldwyn-Mayer. He had also taken over the post of head of the studio. Louis B. Mayer, onetime sponsor of the Andy Hardy series and emphatic spokesman for the "family entertainment" role of motion pictures, had been turned out to pasture, where he occupied himself by grumbling to his friends (with some reason) about the current content of the movies.

Metro's grosses, however, were not outweighing the studio's enormous overhead, and Dore Schary knew he was getting the blame. He had tried to keep things nicely diversified, but this was not enough. Even the musicals were not doing too well. Basically he was still convinced that "tough" subjects were as saleable as musicals.

A property called *Blackboard Jungle* was up for sale. It was a first novel by a young fellow who had spent a few weeks in a New York trade school and collected some stories of violence between pupils and teachers. The novel had been turned down by other studios and independent producers, in some cases specifically because it seemed an irresponsible piece of writing.

M-G-M's production chief didn't see it that way. He thought it was a valuable idea for a message film, just violent enough to put a bomb under public complacency. He bought it and turned it over to his old friend Richard Brooks, now a writer-director at Metro. They thought it might bring in a fairly nice profit if it didn't cost too much to make.

What came out was a frequently believable, tautly directed drama, another in the long line of problem films which found their solutions and their box-office appeal in violent conflict between the good man and the bad man. This time it was a good teacher and a bad pupil.

Blackboard Jungle turned out to be the biggest financial vindication in M-G-M history of Schary's basic belief in problem pictures. Ironically, its success did not seem to delay very much his departure as head of the studio. But it made more money in the domestic market than any other Metro film in 1955. Without more than a moment's hesitation, the company's executives decided they wanted to release it overseas. It was praised by foreign critics as a work of cinematic art and as evidence that Americans didn't pull any punches in criticizing their own way of life. It was condemned by Clare Boothe Luce (then ambassador to Italy) as crudely unrepresentative of American life. Stirred by this extra controversy, moviegoers everywhere flocked to see it.

Nobody knows how many restless young people, in this

country and abroad, absorbed jarring new concepts of insubordination from this single film. The long-term effect of *Blackboard Jungle* on Hollywood, however, is well known. It was followed soon afterward by another picture about high school youth, *Rebel Without a Cause*. Helped immeasurably by the presence of young James Dean in the starring role, the film's theme naturally appealed to all self-righteous adolescents.

Without actually explaining motivations (except by dressing the father in an apron), *Rebel Without a Cause* made the parents the real villains, in accordance with a widely held American attitude. In this case, they had been "running away" from town whenever their boy got in trouble. The film implied that the boy and his friends, if backed up by their elders, could have worked everything out by themselves. It was an interesting theme, though far from adequate (as the rising young star himself was aware). At least it was different from the simpler villain-and-his-friends approach of *Blackboard Jungle*, with its vague assumption of a slum background as cause.

The enormous popularity of these two films put Hollywood producers feverishly on the track of similar themes. Surveys and polls might have gone on for years, vainly claiming the predominance of youth at the box office. But two pictures making real money were immediately persuasive. *The Bad Seed* and *Crime in the Streets* were followed later by *The Strange One* and *The Young Stranger*. The persistence of the cycle at lower levels, once it got under way, was astonishing. Some of the titles are almost unbelievable: *Girls in Prison, The Flaming Teen-Age, Hot Rod Girl, Rumble on the Docks, The Delinquents, Dragstrip Girl, Hot Rod Rumble, Motorcycle Gang, Reform School Girl, Untamed Youth, Young and Dangerous, The Cool and the Crazy, The Cry Baby Killer, Dragstrip Riot, Eighteen and Anxious, High School Confidential, Juvenile Jungle.*

More sex and violence for young people! The quick-buck moviemakers had seen the handwriting on the wall and they had read it fast. Whereas in *Rebel Without a Cause* the love story was both tender and believable, in the formula follow-ups the old-fashioned gangster "moll" became the easiest type to write into the script.

The impact of these teen-age shockers on our mid-century culture is quite incalculable. It may have been slightly softened by the fact that many of the pictures played only the first- and third-run downtown theaters and were ignored by the second-run suburban houses. But the boys and girls who did see them — and sometimes saw them more than once — were the ones who were already rootless, restless, and attracted by the apparently heroic pleasures of crime.

Meanwhile a reviving interest in horror pictures — a peculiar phenomenon which constantly recurs in movie history — began to join up with science fiction themes, which had already had a fairly solid renaissance in the early 1950's. Here again, the titles are almost beyond belief: *Attack of the Crab Monsters, The Cyclops, The*

Deadly Mantis, The Disembodied, The Giant Claw, The Incredible Shrinking Man, The Night the World Exploded, The Undead, Zombies of Mora Tau, The Attack of the Fifty-Foot Woman, The Blob, The Monster from Green Hell, She Gods of the Shark Reef, The Spider, and many, many more.

At one point fantastic fiction and teen-age violence met head-on in a movie everybody thought was a publicist's joke: *I Was a Teen-Age Werewolf.* This was followed by *I Was a Teen-Age Frankenstein, Teen-Age Monster, Teen-Age Caveman,* and *Monster on the Campus.*

By 1959, the cycle began to decline. There were two reasons for this: the slow buildup of parental wrath and the beginning of a decline in box-office receipts for these subjects. The protests finally caused Eric Johnston to agree that Geoffrey Shurlock should call in certain producers and warn them there were just too many teen-age and horror pictures. One of the producers claimed to be surprised that there were so many. Then he said: "Well, they aren't doing so well at the box office anyway." He thereupon canceled a whole group of them.

In a way, of course, the films based on fantastic stories were a swing back to the security of technical innovation as an audience appeal. The death's-head and the atomic machine could be called the same kind of delightfully dizzy gimmick as stereophonic sound or 3-D, and it tended to be considerably cheaper. In this case, however, the audience appeal was considerably narrower.

We may rest assured that the majority of the young people in this country — and among experienced movie fans abroad — are quite familiar with films and with formulas. They can shrug off much of the crime they have been seeing as simply "entertainment." Nor are they easily frightened — even at the age of eight — after the third or fourth "horror" picture, with its obvious rehash of mechanical terrorizers. Some psychoanalysts, paraphrasing Aristotle, even say this is a good "purging" for them to go through, a catharsis that cuts down their desire for violence, rather than giving them models to live by.

Furthermore, American youth live in a free society in which many other influences are brought to bear on them. Movies are not their only source of information, and most of them can be expected to survive the cycle of delinquency films without too many permanent scars. We may also recall that a great variety of other movies came out during this period. There was delightful entertainment: *The King and I, The Solid Gold Cadillac, The Brave One, Operation Mad Ball, Funny Face, The Happy Road, The Pajama Game, Designing Woman, Gigi, Tom Thumb, North by Northwest, Some Like It Hot, The Shaggy Dog.* There were a good number of significant dramas: *Marty, A Man Called Peter, To Hell and Back, East of Eden, The Friendly Persuasion, Giant, War and Peace, The Ten Commandments, Moby Dick, The Bridge on the River Kwai, Time Limit, Twelve Angry Men, A Face in the*

Crowd, The Defiant Ones, Separate Tables, The Diary of Anne Frank, The Last Angry Man, On the Beach, Middle of the Night.

But all of these disclaimers cannot obscure the fact that the theaters were clogged with cheap horror and attractive juvenile gangsters for about three years. The delinquency cycle is important because it was a conscious effort, like the era of technical gimmicks, to hold a slippery audience. It was almost a "sure thing" to appeal to "the kids," since most of them were already loyal customers anyway. For that reason it is hard to see why the producers and exhibitors worked so hard at it. But like the concurrent era of "adult" subjects (which the youngsters also flocked to see), it was a time of almost frantic concern with sensational content. It was also a time when film makers showed how little they knew about their social responsibilities as communicators protected by the First Amendment.

A purely ideological observer — from Russia or Mars, perhaps — might well be both puzzled and astonished. It looked as if the movie industry had organized a concerted attack on the attitudes of young people, forcing on them a familiarity with violence and an appetite for it. Warning the young audience (as an afterthought in the last reel) that punishment might come, they nevertheless exhibited for eighty or more minutes beforehand the glamour and excitement of violence.

Of course it was not so bad as that — not so self-conscious or intentional. Yet the producers did know what they were making. The bright young independents knew they were turning out dubious stuff as a way of getting their first profits. The distributors knew what they were distributing. The exhibitors knew they were exhibiting, over and over again, a way of life quite unlike what they envisioned for their own children.

The reason for all this was that there was another value at stake — the preservation of a system of theaters and of distribution in the face of the competition of television. This was not more important than the welfare of youth. Not one of the desperate theater owners would say that. But the prospect of financial decline was more immediately dangerous, in their eyes, and more measurable, than anything that might happen to youth.

If this new kind of subject matter made fast money at the box office, no other measurement needed to be made. In the democracy of capitalism, the consumer is the voter. If parents came home from work so tired that they wanted to be left in peace in front of their TV sets, the theater owners would have to offer the young people what they obviously liked to see.

After all, movie exhibitors could not be concerned with things like the content of communication or the education of children. They were just businessmen, fighting for their lives. Only a few of them saw that, in their terror, they might be cutting their own throats. Only a few of them realized that the role of film in civilization had some connection with the young moviegoers who were slicing up the theater seats.

Adultery for the Whole Family?

Ten years ago Gilbert Seldes took Hollywood movie-makers to task for pretending to appeal to "The Great Audience," when actually they were appealing only to that limited part of the audience made up of immature young people. He called for more maturity in film making and suggested that this was the only way to get the majority audience of adults back into the theaters.

Hollywood seems to have been following his advice. Thanks to television, Otto Preminger, the U.S. Supreme Court, Brigitte Bardot, and the increasing frankness of the modern novel, American theatrical film makers have been buying and producing more and more stories with "adult themes."

There are at least two drawbacks, however.

In the first place, adultery is not the same thing as maturity. Just because a bedroom comedy or a tragic soap opera deals "frankly" with some of the possibilities of extramarital sex, this doesn't mean that the treatment of the subject has an adult viewpoint. The Code now allows heroes and heroines to suffer very much less over their lapses, and this is closer to some people's actual experience. But maturity is a matter of style and approach. As Mr. Seldes so clearly stated ten years ago, maturity "does not necessarily imply either the tragic sense of life or an excessive sophistication."

Perhaps the most difficult challenge in the art of film making is that rare kind of story which is based on the deepest simplicities of life — on achievement, love, or joy. *Ballad of a Soldier* was that kind of story, and it is sad to realize that there was nothing to compare with this poignant Russian film in the whole line-up of U.S. production in 1960, from *Pollyanna* to *Butterfield 8*.

Again, it takes a special, steady maturity to make motion pictures intended for younger children, as the British have done for years. Except for a brief period in Disney's career, Hollywood has never attempted to do it. American pictures are vaguely intended "for the whole family." This used to mean that they were made to satisfy the twelve-year-old mind of all ages. Now the appeal is more nearly to the fourteen-year-old mind, preoccupied with self and sex.

And this is the second drawback in the new wave of "adult" films. The new subject matter may seem to be elaborately planned to rouse the interest of jaded, stay-at-home adults. But the movies are still playing primarily to kids, and the producers know it. Therefore the stories must be provocative, but in a slick and simplified way, instead of coping honestly with the tricky complexities of human relations. The boys and girls find both *The World of Suzie Wong* and *Where the Boys Are* at the neighborhood theater — and the treatment of Oriental prostitution is not so very different from the treatment of American youth at the beach.

The headlong rush of American youngsters toward pseudosophistication at an ever earlier age is a familiar trend, and movies aren't the only cause of it. The whole public attitude toward the arts is far more permissive than it used to be. Standards of behavior in private life are also much less stringent. The result is a new kind of reverse conformity.

Many people, having studied Freud — by themselves, or in college — now think of sex as something to be encouraged rather than restrained. They think of uninhibited aggression as much less dangerous than feelings of guilt which might restrain aggression. They think of self-discipline for others' sake as a false, Puritanical kind of responsibility. Any kind of censorship, of course, is anathema to these psychologists of unrestraint, and particularly any opposition to a free and full awareness of the Freudian view of the primary role of sex in human life. The science of human relations, still in its observational stage (whether clinical or statistical), reinforces the anti-Puritan trend. So does the whole dominant modern faith in physical science as an objective study. So does the quite different tradition of literary freedom and freedom of speech.

The effects on the arts are well known to most observers. They range from the increasing use of profanity to chapter-long examinations of the sex act. The catalogue of perversions to which the dramatists are driven, in search of more "freedom," is now in danger of running out altogether.

But there is a very large proportion of the population which does not accept the total-immersion theory of sex and sex education. Many parents feel that their children need not necessarily be flooded with "adult" experiences before they even reach their teens. They are convinced that education is in many respects a gradual process — that children have a right to be children for a while and enjoy the natural, unhurried growth which can be the basis for solid maturity.

It is easy enough to say, "Well, that's the parents' decision, the parents' responsibility." In reality the family is a weak minority among the jarring forces brought to bear on today's youth. Can a mother and father compete with sex education at school, the groundswell of "other-directed" faddism in young peoples' groups, the tell-it-all paperbacks and magazines, and on top of that the easy availability of "adult" movies?

Even the most responsible family finds it a losing proposition to stand against the local exhibitor and his vested interest in young people. Obviously the folks are not going to go to all the movies themselves, and then recommend certain ones to the children afterward. How can mother know what's really in that picture at the Grand? How can father know that the parents' groups recommended the last six pictures only for "adults and mature young people"? Mother knows you can't tell anything by the advertising. Father hasn't time to call up the PTA. And there is no really accepted community process, no familiar label, by which movies can be sorted out.

Classification of films is the most talked-about solution to this mounting problem. It is also the most sensible solution. Most of the other countries of the world have some form of labeling. Usually this labeling is done by a public or semi-public agency. The French are perpetually astonished that Americans permit motion picture theaters to sell tickets indiscriminately to children. In England, American film distributors must submit to classification like everybody else, and sometimes the limiting "X" label in the advertisements is actually profitable, because it brings in more of the adult audience Mr. Seldes was talking about.

Classification has already begun, in a small way, in this country. Adult tags have been applied to a number of foreign films. Hollywood distributing companies have used adult labels occasionally. But these have been more or less voluntary decisions, indifferently enforced by theaters, and never uniform throughout the country or throughout the period of release.

There is increasing public pressure for official action. Since the 5-4 decision of the Supreme Court in the Times Film Company case — which for the first time put a stamp of approval on the idea of censorship prior to release — censorship bills have multiplied in state legislatures. Many of these bills specifically call for a classification system under some state or local authority.

The Times Film decision will very likely be overturned by the Supreme Court, or at least carefully circumscribed in its effect, since it seems to contradict most of the precedents on freedom of speech. But the decision itself can be interpreted in part as a reaction against the recent crop of movies. It may be that Supreme Court justices neither read the election returns nor go to the movies. But they do have children and friends. Between the lines, the decision seems to say: Something has to be done about films.

All this follows the historical pattern of pressure on Hollywood. The Production Code was accepted by the industry only because of the threat of both federal and state censorship in 1929-30. Four years later, the requirement of a Production Code seal for every picture — and a $25,000 penalty for nonconformity — was accepted by the industry only because of the threat of boycott by the newly formed Catholic Legion of Decency. In 1960 and 1961, the National Council of Churches was more outspoken than ever before on the subject of films, but again it was the Legion of Decency which found a way to make pressure effective by enforcing privately what amounted to a classification system. A clear label, "For Adults Only," had to appear in all advertising for *Elmer Gantry* if it was to avoid condemnation by the Legion. Hollywood has two ways to adjust, under this system — by accepting the "adult" label or by accepting changes in the film.

The Production Code office is as qualified as anybody to undertake the service of classification. Hollywood producers will object at first. They will worry about the box office. They will protest, in the proud new legal language which permits them (since the *Miracle* case) to wrap themselves in the First Amendment and claim freedom of speech for the screen. But they will finally accept classification, because it is better than censorship. In fact, classification can prevent excesses of censorship, because a strong system of censorship without classification tends to prohibit everything except what is suitable for children.

It would be unfortunate if the system selected were to permit only two categories — "adult" and "unrestricted." The intermediate scheme, which allows young people "if accompanied by an adult," would not only give parents an incentive to go to the movies more often. It would also give them an opportunity to share the experience of their children so that they can actually fulfill their responsibilities in that gray area of education enforced by the everpresence of mass communication. Through discussion and criticism of the ways of life presented in Hollywood movies — and foreign movies — parents can find contact points for family understanding which would be denied them if they always went to their own separate movies at the art houses. Parental concern can be positive as well as negative, and the community would profit immensely if parents had a chat with the theater owner once in a while.

American exhibitors are against classification, and the Motion Picture Association has so far accepted their position. In their eyes, no doubt, every child turned away from the box office is being denied a fundamental right Americans have always enjoyed. But times have changed, and so have the movies. Now it is clear that there is another, conflicting duty to be considered: the duty of society to lay down the broad outlines of the education of children.

There is nothing in the First Amendment which gives every ten-year-old the constitutional right to see *Suddenly Last Summer*.

4

INDEPENDENCE WITH A VENGEANCE

"Let actors act, directors direct, and producers produce."

Samuel Goldwyn

INDEPENDENT production has been hailed as a kind of cure-all for what ails Hollywood, both artistically and commercially. It has been praised as a source of new freedom, new talent, and new ideas.

But the change-over from the old studio system is more apparent than real. And when independence does have some independence about it, the films that emerge are as likely to appeal to the lowest common denominator of taste as they did in the old days.

Independent production, like the Pay-TV of the future, is only as good as the people involved in it and the financial arrangements surrounding it.

Agents and Actors Become Producers

Independence has long been a sturdy tradition in the ever-changing movie industry. Rebellion against monopoly began in the first years of the silents, when Adolph

Zukor (later a monopolist in his own way) defied the Motion Picture Patents Company by showing the four-reel *Queen Elizabeth*, starring Sarah Bernhardt, at the Lyceum Theater in New York. United Artists, from its very beginning, in 1919, represented actors and directors who wanted to be free of "front office interference" in selecting stories. Cecil B. deMille, Samuel Goldwyn, David O. Selznick, and Stanley Kramer are only the most famous of the intractables who have insisted on their own way of working. The Society of Independent Motion Picture Producers was, until 1958, an active organization on the Hollywood scene; its decline to a nominal entity, without an executive director, is one of the paradoxes of the post-television era.

The most recent pattern of independent operation stemmed in part from the rebirth of United Artists in 1951, under Arthur Krim and Robert Benjamin. These vigorous young lawyers and their able vice-president Max Youngstein (also a lawyer) took over the basic notion of autonomous responsibility for production, already characteristic of United Artists. They added a free-wheeling willingness to take on a variety of product, good and bad, to keep up their volume of distribution. They realized that part of what ailed the major companies was over-head — that is, the cost of maintaining big stages and back lots and expensive specialized staffs. They also realized that big tax advantages could be offered to film makers who were willing to organize independent corporations and give up the security of studio salaries. They reminded their partners-in-independence that no studio "czar" would look at their rushes and tell them how to make their pictures. They had, at the right moment, the notable and profitable assistance of Sam Spiegel and John Huston, who made *The African Queen,* and Stanley Kramer and Fred Zinnemann, who made *High Noon.* They transformed a dying organization into a moneymaking enterprise within two years.

Hollywood is always impressed by success, and the U.A. story was just about the only encouraging sign on the horizon in the early days of TV. Perhaps the answer was to have no actual investment in sound stages or in other real estate devoted to production. Perhaps the best thing, after all, was to have an office and a telephone, seek money, buy stories, negotiate with stars, and (when production was imminent) simply rent somebody else's real estate.

At the same time, TV's competition began to force new policies in the major companies. The realization finally dawned that the place of the theatrical film in American life was changing. This conviction grew more and more dominant as wide-screen systems won favor and small theaters continued to disappear. Hollywood observers and even some Hollywood spokesmen began to predict that the motion picture for theaters would eventually find its place as a special event, located on the consumer's calendar somewhere between the rarity of a legitimate stage production and the frequency of TV. Fewer and "better" pictures were to be the answer to competition.

(*Around the World in 80 Days* later became a favorite example. It was special and big — and Mike Todd was very independent.)

The familiar system of production in major studios began to break down. Top actors and directors were spending too much time cooling their heels in Beverly Hills or Malibu, comfortably drawing their salaries, while fewer and fewer properties were being okayed for production. As the studios cut down production plans, they also began to cut back on contract lists. This applied to lesser-known and lower-paid people, too. No longer would there be a long-term pattern of training youngsters by putting them in minor roles in second-string films. There weren't any second-string films, at least judging by the budgets. The youngsters would have to get their experience in television.

The major stars, presumably, were rich enough and high-priced enough not to care about contracts any more. This proved to be the case. One by one, they vanished from the major lots, some of them agreeing to come back for one or two pictures a year. But because the stars were now free to negotiate, their agreements began to cost a great deal more.

They knew what they were doing, and so did their agents. Already James Stewart had shown how far a free-lance actor could go in a deal with a major studio if he gambled on his box-office power. For his role in *Winchester 73* his agent demanded — and got for him — 50 per cent of the net profits. Danny Kaye reportedly got

$250,000 and 10 per cent of the profits for his appearance in *White Christmas.*

For those at the top, free-lancing had irresistible charms. Clark Gable could hardly wait to be free of his twelve-year-old contract at Metro. Paul Newman signed a seven-year deal with Warners and within two years regretted it bitterly. Marilyn Monroe caught the fever of independence and managed to have her way.

As actors' earnings rose into higher brackets, tax lawyers advised new administrative arrangements. If the stars set up their own companies, much of their income could be listed under capital gains, rather than as personal salaries, and they could keep a lot more of what they got. A name on a door, a secretary, a telephone, a fee to a corporation lawyer, and the actor (and his agent) were in business. They could go looking for scripts like anybody else, and after that, hire a director, a crew, and a sound stage. They could release through United Artists or through any major company.

The agent became the key man in many production decisions. The three top talent agencies (William Morris, Music Corporation of America, and Famous Artists) had long been diversified — that is, instead of devoting themselves exclusively to actors or writers, they had set up separate but coordinated departments for actors, writers, directors, producers. Now it was more than ever obvious that combination was the clue to success. Instead of offering a script (or a writer) to a studio which already had a contract list of actors, or offering an actor to a studio well staffed with writers, the agency would offer a combination — a "package." This usually consisted of a writer and his script, one or two stars, and even a director. Sometimes the "package" was already an independent corporation. The studio would have to take it or leave it.

All the studio could offer in exchange was (1) a physical plant and some technical departments, (2) a sales apparatus for distributing films to theaters, and (3) a familiarity with the mysteries of procuring money. All of these advantages could eventually be replaced by a hustling independent company, now that the stars — the main lever for extracting money — were available for independent deals. Harold Hecht and Burt Lancaster, the first and most notable of the agent-actor combinations, proved this by becoming within two years a production team with a substantial list of critical and box-office successes behind them. They released their pictures through United Artists.

The talent agent's part in the changing scene of independent production has had two very significant effects. In the first place, he has helped to make everything cost more. Because his job is to get more money for his clients and his own fee is proportionally based on the money his clients get, the agent is normally quite unconcerned with the total cost of a picture. He is primarily concerned with the value of his client's services.

The price of a client is a matter of almost magical manipulation of opinions and impressions. The difference

between a star salary of $100,000 per picture and
$150,000 per picture is impossible to explain rationally.
John Wayne and William Holden were promised by the
producers of *The Horse Soldiers* a guarantee of $750,000
apiece. There is nothing reasonable about such a figure.
If Elizabeth Taylor gets $1,000,000 for appearing as Cleo-
patra, the picture may make enough money to pay such a
fee in the long run, but it is based on the first instance on
finely charged emotion and calculated bluff. Sometimes,
of course, the bluff is based primarily on the emotions of
the star, who reads the trade papers like everyone else
and doesn't want to be left behind in the salary spiral.
From Mary Pickford to Cary Grant, there have always
been stars with a knack for getting and keeping money.
But it's up to the agent to make the arrangements.

The agent is a poker player. He is expected to think
along a single track, one transaction at a time, pointing
toward the largest possible stack of chips — from which
he periodically withdraws his own 10 per cent. The agent
is therefore concerned with the over-all management of a
picture only when his client has a profit participation in
lieu of salary, and even then his primary interest is in
protecting the price of his client for the next picture. He
has little interest in a five-year plan.

This, then, is the second effect of the expanded role of
talent agents. Long-range plans, either for talent or for
a program of pictures, have become rare and almost ac-
cidental. In the old days, under the major studio system,
a hard-fisted paternal character like L. B. Mayer or Harry

Cohn could plan a developing career for a new young star or director because he had him under contract. Independence is different — far more insecure for the individual with talent. The agent's role has become all-important.

The agent, however, is not necessarily a producer. He has power over individual actors and writers, but that power may be fleeting, for an artist can change his agent. He must exercise his power quickly when the actor needs a job. He has the power of ideas, of preparing "packages" for independents, but these are usually "one-shot deals." Although there are many responsible agents who are smart enough to worry about their client's long-term interests, the agent — by nature and by function — is not a responsible film maker. It is not his business to worry about whether the box-office receipts will cover costs and profits. He may have time to think, between phone calls, "Jimmy Smith has been in too many westerns lately. We ought to put him with Hitchcock, or maybe he's ready for a musical for a change." He does not have time — nor is he in a position — to think about his actor's development as part of a program of production.

A troubled actor, eager for quick approval, is even less likely to be a long-range planner. Restive under the old paternalism of the studio executives, he often felt he wanted to run his own life. But now the independent, "incorporated" actor is forced to make day-to-day decisions for immediate profit, based on his own or his agent's estimate of the script at hand and what the audience presumably wants at the moment. He naturally tends to accept roles which give him immediate big opportunities rather than solid development.

What happens when an agent actually turns into a producer, with direct responsibility for a film or a series of films? This paradox has bothered Hollywood for nearly ten years. The agent-producer represents the performer or writer or director, on the one hand, as a salesman for an employee's services. On the other hand, he is joining with the future employee in a new role as an employer. He sells somebody to himself and pockets a fee for it.

This anomalous relationship was actually encouraged by the Screen Actors Guild by a special waiver in a contract with the Artists' Managers Guild in 1954. It all started with TV films. The uncharted land rush of TV film making seemed most likely to be prosperously seeded if MCA and other talent agencies could be unleashed to roam free and wild — "packaging" as they went. When the Actors Guild finally announced, in 1961, that actors' agents could not be permitted, after June 1962, to be actors' employers too, many of the agent-producers decided to stop being agents and took up producing full time. The major executives at MCA have moved over to the former subsidiary company, Revue Productions, where the profits are many times larger.

This may put a new look on the face of things. Nobody can tell which of these middlemen will survive the metamorphosis into creative decision makers. There is a good chance, however, that their longer range responsibility for

programs of production may result in a decline in the
heady freedom of independence.

The Cautious Independent Chooses Terror

It is fruitless to try to generalize about the baffling variety of types and conditions "independence" assumes
in Hollywood. Every contract — annual or per picture
— is a little different. At one extreme, a producer may
have no more autonomy than before he signed a new deal
with the studio; he sits at the same desk and looks over
the same scripts sent to him by the story department, but
he gets proportionately more money if the picture he
makes makes more money. At the other extreme is the
producer who buys an option on a script himself and per-
suades both the banks and the stars to have faith in him.
The range of arrangements between the extremes is wide
enough to keep a small army of lawyers alert and busy.
But it is clear that many producers are still only as free
as their production-distribution deal lets them be.

Obviously there were plenty of disadvantages under
the centralized control of the old studio system. The
staff producer had to film the stories the company executives bought. He had to work within the limits of toler-
ance of the executive in charge of production. He might
be hemmed in by the veterans in the art department or
the cutting rooms. He had to use players on contract at
the studio, and he had no control over advertising or
publicity. But even within the traditional system, a well-

known director like William Wyler or George Stevens
had considerable freedom to maneuver, to accept or re-
ject distasteful projects.

An independent may think he is freer, but he will
shortly discover that his hands are tied in new ways. In
the first place, United Artists is no longer so very different from any of the so-called major studios. The producer or director is reasonably free once his subject or
script is accepted, but increasingly the range of acceptable
subjects is limited to the usual costly, pre-sold projects.
In the second place, his chances of producing a work of
art are actually diminished by the unique, unforeseen red
tape of independence.

For the struggling producer who is at least half free —
a man who is not himself an actor or an agent and who
likes to think he has long-range plans for a program of
stories — independence sometimes becomes almost in-
tolerable. He sees his present script as having a certain
balance and point of view. But in order to get the people
he wants, he must compromise among so many "free"
agents and owners that his script is in ribbons, his patience in tatters, and his best plans go down the drain.
The actor and the actor's agent will disagree with the
producer and with each other on the lines and the action
in the "big scene." The director will insist upon handling
the ending a different way. The distributor (when the
producer finally does sign a contract) is likely to be, after
all, a major company, and several studio executives will
get into the act before negotiations are over. The pro-

ducer's proud epic will be changed drastically in the editing room. It will then be sold as the lower half of a double bill in three hundred situations simultaneously with no appropriations for advance publicity. By this time, "independence" has become a misnomer and a mockery.

The universal fear of the box office is what makes the red tape bind so tightly for the truly independent producer. The same psychological hurdle faced the staff producer in the studio, but for the independent it is more immediate, more everpresent, and far more intense.

The long, thin line of independents is made up of men who are all trying bravely to think like studios. But they haven't the defense in depth to act like studios. Each producer is right up there on the firing line, with his one picture, on which everything depends. He may have his money for this one, but he's got to make it back — and big — or he won't get it next time. If he isn't a rugged individual, he won't survive. Being an artist has little to do with it.

So what is the safest thing for him to do? According to the advertising writers, the subjects with the broadest attention-getting appeal are sex and violence. His first picture, then, will probably be a western or a crime picture, just to be safe — something like *Little Caesar* or *Asphalt Jungle* or *Stagecoach*, only cheaper. He has to deliver a winner the first time. He can't say to himself: "I've got four pictures going and the one I'm not sure of will be paid for by the others." He can't even say: "I'm not sure which one I'm not sure of, but surely one of the four will be a winner!" His program, if any, is spaced out into the dim future.

Then, the second time around, if he has succeeded well enough to stay on the merry-go-round, he decides to do the same thing over again, just to be safe.

If he isn't a little careless, he may go on doing this forever. If he is careful, he may decide that there is never quite enough money to go out on a limb and do that wonderful story he has been holding in reserve.

The effect of independence on the themes chosen by younger theatrical film makers is spread on the record at the Production Code Administration. According to Geoffrey Shurlock, the first film by a new independent company, time after time, is a story of violence. Stanley Kubrick was careful to begin his Hollywood movie-directing career with *The Killing*. Even Sam Goldwyn, Jr., who might be expected to feel secure, started producing films, as it happened, with *Man with a Gun*. Hecht-Lancaster could not undertake to make *Marty* until after they were already a Major Independent, with some westerns nicely stacked up in the till. The fact that *Marty* made a tremendous amount of money in comparison to its inconsiderable cost has made no difference in the traditional way of thinking. *Marty* is still called a "fluke."

There has been sporadic talk of a "new wave" of young film makers in America, as a result of all the talk about the "nouvelle vague" in France. Most of the talk is based on wishful thinking. Perhaps somebody with pol-

ished skills and untarnished vision will emerge to great-
ness from the smokescreen of the "exploitation pictures"
that accompanied the rise of independence in 1956-59 —
from among the people who worked on pictures like
*Born Reckless, City of Fear, Cry Tough, The Fearmakers,
Go, Johnny, Go, High School Big Shot, Riot in Juvenile
Prison, Speed Crazy, Teen Age Thunder, Vice Raid,*
and *Gang War.* It seems more likely that this particular
wave will drift into the formulas of TV film making or
vanish altogether.

The young men the eastern critics have been trying to
discover seem to consist of Leslie Stevens, who made the
sex shocker, *Private Property,* and John Cassavetes, who
did a nonscripted picture called *Shadows,* with the possible addition of Robert Radnitz, who began his producing in highly unorthodox manner with the old-fashioned
childhood story, *The Dog of Flanders.* More promising,
perhaps, is the fact that Denis and Terry Sanders, graduates of UCLA's theater arts department, managed to
finish a picture for United Artists called *War Hunt,* and
Irvin Kershner, an alumnus of the USC Cinema Department, was signed in 1962 to direct low-budget pictures for
the Mirisch Company.

But one or two low-budget films don't make a wave.
What brilliant beginners need is the protection of a tol-
erant system and a stimulating environment. They need
guidance within freedom — and freedom not only from
excessive paternalism but also from the paralyzing red
tape of multiple ownership of each project.

The financial environment is all against the experimental newcomer. Theater men say they need "product," but except for the horror and crime stories, they usually shy away from pictures without established stars — and stars are by far the biggest element of cost. Every other major cost is going steadily up. The guilds and unions press for new advantages every year. Since the International Alliance of Theatrical and Stage Employees contains both the theatrical projectionists and the production unions, a non-union picture has little chance of being shown in an American theater. While the shortage of product makes this rule much less binding now, it certainly acts to prevent the making of low-budget independent films. Perhaps the best and cheapest way for a young American producer or director to be "discovered" is to shoot a 16-millimeter film in South America without professional actors and win a prize at a European film festival.

In France, the thirty or forty new young directors (some of them not so young) have been fortified by a decade of talk and criticism, led by the late editor-critic, André Bazin; they have been fed with motion picture history at the film showings of the Cinémathèque in Paris. There is no such concentrated intellectual activity going on in the United States among present and future film makers. Until the film companies, the film museums, and the university film departments get together in some new way, there will be no such groundwork for creativity in this country.

There is almost no long-term investment in young people in Hollywood. Independent producers are sometimes willing to take on a bright young production assistant, and such a beginner can "get in" somewhat more easily to work on an independent film, because budgets and supervision are not as rigid outside the studios. But a young man has to be very bright and agile to know where to go after that first job. For the most part, Hollywood seems to be depending on its second generation. Sons of executives, like Plato Skouras and Richard Zanuck, or sons of directors, like George Stevens, Jr., happen to be wise and decent and promising young men. But there is hardly a rebel among them.

The big-money system of independent bargaining has been no great breath of fresh air, no wide open door to the expression of individuality by directors suddenly freed of studio trammels. There are few new directors at all, except those trained in the remarkable freedom of the early days of live television — men like Delbert Mann, Sidney Lumet, John Frankenheimer, or Robert Mulligan.

A Touch of Paternalism in a No Man's Land?

The current kind of costly independence has freed a few top producer-directors to do almost as they please. It has bought Otto Preminger a ticket to the Michigan woods for *Anatomy of a Murder* and to Israel for *Exodus*. It has restored Billy Wilder to the pleasures of comedy.

It finally gave William Wyler the chance to make *The Friendly Persuasion*. It sent Sam Spiegel to the waterfront and the river Kwai and gave other opportunities to Elia Kazan and David Lean. These are no small gains. We can be pleased with them without at the same time being misled into calling the situation either a universal revolution of freedom or the best pattern for all moviemaking everywhere from now on.

Can we detect, after all, any infallible and overwhelming differences between independent and studio productions over the last few years? Was *Marty* really so much better than *East of Eden*, for example? Was *The Pride and the Passion* better than *Ben-Hur*? Was *Patterns* so much more honest or outspoken than *Executive Suite*? Was *Pork Chop Hill* a better war picture than *Battleground*? Was *Some Like It Hot* funnier than *Born Yesterday*?

Of course it is impossible to find a basis for comparison for films so widely separated in time. But if any close critical analysis were possible, relating motion pictures to their time and to their system of production, I doubt very much whether the Hollywood films of the last five years would appear to be of outstanding quality as compared with the years before that. Nor do I think the strictly studio films would suffer drastically in contrast. There would probably be, as the social scientists say, no statistically reliable difference. (Of course there would be no statistically reliable critics in the first place.)

The freedom of the independent is sometimes defended as having broken down some of the restrictions of the Production Code. Certainly we can find in recent pictures more casualness in the use of words and far more explicitness in sexual relationships. But this cannot be primarily attributed to any special system of production. It is a reflection of the temper of the times, the competition of television, and the example of foreign films.

The narcotics issue, to be sure, was first brought up by an independent. Mr. Preminger's achievement was a mixed blessing, at best, but was *The Man with the Golden Arm* so much better than the studio film, *A Hatful of Rain* — or even *The Lost Weekend,* an earlier studio production which dealt harshly with the problems of alcoholism?

Independence has always been an important source of path-breaking ideas and leadership in Hollywood. Originality and daring are the proud privileges of independent producers in any year or any era. But the credit for whatever is good among the films of the last five years must go to the stubbornly creative men who have learned to work with the new system and fight its limitations, just as they coped with the problems of the wide screen. They have continued to search for stories of quality; they have held on to high standards of talent and production. Strong and artistic individuals will make great pictures, whatever the production system.

This latest kind of independence puts a premium on toughness, not talent. Some of the best potential contributors to the film medium, however, are not strong enough to make their contributions by themselves. They need the right kind of paternalism — the right kind of faith in their special potentialities — the kind of guidance the executive producer system sometimes gives. If there are to be future Thomas Wolfes of the screen, they will need more than one Maxwell Perkins to discipline and guide them.

Art is achieved in the first instance only by individuals. Its carry-over into the completed complexity of a motion picture can happen only with the help of many other individuals and groups who have accepted the intentions of the artists who started the process. Only great art, conceived by writers and realized by directors, can light the spark that catches the heart and achieves the chain reaction of critical and box-office success so fervently desired by moviemakers and public alike.

A production system is valuable only so far as it makes that miracle of communication happen. The producer may be independent; he may be on a studio staff or an executive in charge of other producers. He may be a silent partner or an active participant in the writing and directing processes. But he is a superfluous and irrelevant figure — a mere financial cog or a frustrated bundle of will power — unless he is strong enough and patient enough to provide real freedom for the art of film making, unless he takes the opportunity and has the ability to discover, pursue, protect, encourage, chasten, and reward the talent that lights the spark.

It is time for Hollywood to take another look at the

advantages and disadvantages of independent production. It is time to think whether the development of a few strong centers of responsibility for programs of films might not be a revitalizing factor in the current history of American motion pictures. The flight to foreign shores and the frantic preoccupation with pre-sold best sellers — both of them dominant trends in Hollywood — stem in part from the compulsion to make every single film a "blockbuster." This compulsion, so characteristic of the independent's insecurity, might be tempered and balanced if executive producers became fashionable again.

If Pay-TV arrives, the immediate demand for quantity production ("Every year," Jerry Wald predicts, "365 brand-new stories!") may cue the reappearance of executive producers who must quickly find and cultivate new writers and directors. Like the Irving Thalberg period in the transition to sound or the Fred Coe period when transcontinental TV brought "intimate drama" into the living room, the very haste of Pay-TV to fill new needs may avoid for a while the dullness of conformity to some imagined audience taste — may avoid the bureaucracy of decision making which cramps the artists with conformity. But unless there are strong centers of creative leadership and some financial centralization, here and there, that dares to continue supporting programs of varied themes and appeals, the excitement of a new distribution system will soon decline into the same old sameness — the conformity that widespread fear of the public always induces.

Every studio still has a chief of production, but such men are primarily negotiators, occupied with contracts, agents, and the crises of worldwide production. They have little time for the slow processes of artistic leadership or the encouragement of reluctant talent. There is a hint of a possible future pattern in the Mirisch Company, with its partnership arrangements involving Fred Zinnemann, William Wyler, Billy Wilder, and Robert Wise. Stanley Kramer has recently undertaken several films using younger directors. John Houseman manages to keep at least two film projects going at once at M-G-M. But the creative executive can have only limited freedom or power as long as the myth of independence dominates the Hollywood scene.

Irving Thalberg was still relatively young and unknown when he left Universal Pictures to be Louis B. Mayer's vice-president in charge of production. He was not a tough guy. He was small and soft-spoken, and he depended on the protection of the front office. He had a long-term contract, an instinctive understanding of the film medium, and an extraordinary ability to encourage talented people. He would have found it impossible to work in the no man's land of independent competition. He was enough of a fighter to protect his own position (for a long time) and to protect the talented people he attracted to him. But he didn't have to budget and buy every major artistic contribution to every film on the basis of giving away partial ownership and a voice in every decision.

5

HOLLYWOOD FACES THE WORLD

"A tree is a tree, a rock is a rock: shoot it in Griffith Park!"

Old Hollywood proverb

MID-CENTURY movie making has gone global. Hollywood is no longer even a geographical expression. It is a state of mind, operating worldwide. It is a starlet at Cannes and a producer on location in Rome. It is Ava Gardner, who lives in Spain, and Bill Holden, who has moved to Switzerland. It is a novelist at work on a screenplay in London and a screenwriter at work on a novel in Hawaii.

Hollywood has always been seen through many eyes — by a moviegoer in Bombay, a banker-stockholder in England, a theater owner in Peru. Its worldwide impact was great even in the silent days.

Now the impact is being felt in reverse. Hollywood still influences the world, but the world is also becoming a factor to reckon with in Hollywood. Foreign markets are no longer merely dumping grounds for films that have already made their profits. Foreign receipts are no longer merely "gravy." They are more than 50 per cent of the gross.

This has direct effects on plans for film making in Hollywood. The democracy of the box office — not the anxious advice of diplomats and editorial writers — has begun to convince America's film companies that many of their decisions must be considered from an international point of view.

This also means that the film producer is no longer restricted to satisfying American audiences. He is free to find his money anywhere in the world. The standards of Boston or Chicago need not deter him very much. American problems of urbanism or education or segregation or traffic are not of much interest to him if he doesn't think they will interest the foreign audience. He is a worldwide communicator and he reports to nobody but the national censors and the banks.

The Competitive Foreign Market

The facts are not well known, and they are illuminating. At last count, according to the U.S. Department of Commerce, there were 154,852 motion picture theaters in the world. Of this number, only 16,991 are in the United States (4700 of them drive-ins). Here are some comparative figures for other regions and nations (the Soviet figure, here and below, includes mobile 16-millimeter theaters and is therefore greatly inflated):

Europe: 103,990

USSR	45,600	West Germany	6,884
United Kingdom	3,457	East Germany	1,550
France	5,778	Sweden	2,403
Spain	6,080	Italy	10,508

Other European countries 21,730

Mexico and Central America	2,927	Far East	15,697
		Middle East	694
South America	6,973	Africa	2,168
Caribbean	857	Atlantic Islands	216
Canada	1,727	South Pacific	2,311

Audience statistics tell more about the actual impact of films, since theaters vary greatly in size. But even the estimates of audience potential must be viewed with caution, since theater men are fond of rounding off numbers upward. The number of theater seats in four-wall theaters in the United States is only 11,300,000 of the 73,826,349 in the world.

Europe: 42,863,551

USSR:	17,000,000	West Germany	2,843,963
United Kingdom	3,450,000	East Germany	550,000
France	2,785,655	Sweden	600,000
Spain	3,663,000	Italy	4,700,000

Other European countries 7,270,933

Mexico and Central America	2,025,723	Far East	7,918,969
		Middle East	451,000
South America	4,518,187	Africa	1,459,760
Caribbean	592,226	Atlantic Islands	97,173
Canada	810,000	South Pacific	1,463,710

Since 1955, the number of theater seats has increased by 35 per cent in Africa and in Europe, by 43 per cent in the Far East, and by 63 per cent in the Middle East.

Competition among nations has always been a factor in international film distribution, but the extent of it has ebbed and flowed with technological change. In the silent days, of course, motion pictures moved freely across boundaries. Only the occasional printed titles had to be changed from one language to another — and some of the best German films of the early 1920's had few titles to change.

The coming of sound raised language barriers too steep for any but the most outstanding films to surmount. Printed titles had to be burned right into the face of the photography. This was all right for the enthusiasts in the slowly growing number of "art theaters." But not until the skill of "dubbing in" voices reached a level slightly above embarrassment could translated films reach a mass audience in other countries. The development of dubbing skills made it easier for American films to reach foreign audiences, at least in those countries which would accept this technique. The process has been used by the major companies for many years. On the other hand, dubbing can also make it easier for a small country with a small film industry to seek wider distribution. Because of the growing popularity of foreign films, dubbed sound tracks have recently become much more common in this country.

With wider distribution, foreign films can have bigger

budgets. With bigger budgets, a small country can turn out product more like Hollywood's. This means the loss of individuality, artistry, and even identity — and eventually a falling-off in world interest in the small country's films, once they lose their unique background and atmosphere. But the immediate chance for more profits and bigger budgets is hard to resist.

Italian producers have been especially active in seeking world markets during the decade since early low-budget film makers like Rossellini and DeSica made a name for Italian films. Competing in their own country with TV sets in the cafés, competing both at home and overseas with the big-screen products of Hollywood, the Italians have put less emphasis on competition and more on "co-production." This new financial invention means the sharing of costs and stars with American or French or British companies, and after that, a mutual sharing of markets. Paramount found it useful for *War and Peace* and many lesser subjects since. Co-production is a good way for American companies, too, to enlarge film budgets, expand audiences, and generally soften the blows of competition in the world arena.

Motion picture production is being seriously undertaken in an increasing number of countries. In Sweden, when Ingmar Bergman began making films, his budgets were strictly limited to the national audience he could expect to reach. His astonishing international success proves once more that a unique contribution to film can find a world audience despite language barriers and the supposed illiteracy of audiences. The popularity of Japanese films, based mainly on early directing achievements by Akira Kurosawa (especially *Rashomon*) has been paralleled by the same expanding of production costs and cheapening of content that has occurred in Italy. Japan is now the largest producer of films in the world. Some of the statistics for 1959 feature production are instructive:

Japan	502	U.S.	187	West Germany	100
India	310	Italy	167	Mexico	86
Hong Kong	273	France	136	Spain	68

Since motion pictures are probably the most expensive form of national self-expression, it is noteworthy that we are beginning to see film production come from such countries as Greece, Yugoslavia, Brazil, Argentina, and even Holland. Iron Curtain countries, of course, obeying Lenin's dictum about the importance of films, are busy: Hungary, Bulgaria, Poland, Czechoslovakia, Cuba. Russia has expanded production prodigiously in the years since Stalin's death.

The weekly world audience for American films is estimated by the Film Daily Yearbook to be 200,000,000 people. Of these, only 44,000,000 are in the United States. But foreign audiences pay much less for their tickets. In order to bring in from overseas that other half of every dollar earned, movie distributors must attract *more than three times* as many patrons as they do in this country.

Such figures reveal the box the American box office is in. While the audience abroad is growing larger in proportion to the declining domestic audience, selling pictures in foreign markets is getting harder all the time.

From a combination of factors, it seems clear that America's competitive position in film distribution abroad has declined. Fewer films are being produced by Hollywood companies. More are being made in other countries. In many instances co-production arrangements have blurred American contributions to the final result on the screen. The impact of TV is beginning to be felt, notably in Japan, Great Britain, and western Europe.

Foreign screen time for American films has been proportionately falling, year by year. American films are still more popular than those from any other single country, but if there ever was a danger of a Hollywood monopoly, it no longer exists. Ten years ago, American motion pictures occupied from 80 to 90 per cent of the screen time in foreign theaters. Five years ago this figure was 68 per cent. Today it averages 60 per cent — 60 per cent in England, 50 in Italy, 35 in France, 30 in Germany, 50 in Argentina, 30 in Japan. Recently a handful of current films have been seen for the first time in Russia.

Official restrictions by foreign governments are continually changing and are the subject of endless international conferences. Eric Johnston, president of the Motion Picture Association, is seldom seen in Hollywood. He and his chief lieutenants are overseas much of the time, trying to wring concessions little by little, country by country, from boards of trade, economic commissions, tariff experts, and censors.

The restrictions occur on several levels. In certain countries, like India and Indonesia, the censors are particularly hard on the kind of "action" films Americans like to make. In most countries, there are general limitations like taxes, import duties, and license procedures. In between are the elaborate problems of quotas and "frozen funds."

Quotas are primarily intended to encourage national film production by keeping out more than a certain number of American movies each year. Some countries have no specific import quotas but specify that theaters must include a certain number of nationally produced films or show them during a certain percentage of their screen time.

French authorities, for example, decided that no more than 110 films by major American companies could come in during 1960. These are divided up by the MPA among its members. Independent film-makers have to fight for their own quotas. After all that, of course, each company must still seek out specific theater men and sell the product to them.

The quota system not only encourages national film-making. It tends to discourage American production. If only about 15 pictures from the studio can get into the major markets this year, then there isn't much point in making more than 15. Thus the foreign market, so important to the success of a release schedule, often reduces the American market to strictly secondary consideration. When the decision is between two pictures, one for the

American market and one that can be expected to go well everywhere, the decision is likely to go against the picture for the U.S.

Pressures for Overseas Production

The ingenious notion of blocking or "freezing" American dollars has had a different kind of effect. It has served to force more American producers to make their films abroad.

Although the accounting problems for the film maker may be baffling, the basic concept of frozen funds is simple. The producer makes a picture, distributes it in Japan, and receives only one fourth of his box office in dollars. The rest is in yen, unconverted to dollars, held by the government in a blocked account in Tokyo. It's the producer's money, but all those millions of yen won't buy a single star or story or crew in the United States of America. The answer is to find a project like *Sayonara* that can be done in Japan. The only trouble is that the film made in Japan may then be very popular at the Japanese box office and eventually the frozen funds are bigger than ever.

Motion picture companies found themselves becoming diversified in a hurry as they struggled to get their dollars out of foreign lands. All sorts of schemes have been worked out. American film companies have bought beef in Argentina and polo ponies in Chile. M-G-M used some of its blocked lire to buy Italian marble and sold it to the

Vermont Marble Company. In 1955, the MPA went so far as to advance a $7,500,000 loan to the Japanese government (out of frozen yen), repayable in dollars in three to seven years.

Recently film companies willing to produce in foreign countries have been confronted with a carrot as well as a stick. Special subsidies for national film production in England, France, and elsewhere have been interpreted to apply also to co-production arrangements with American companies, if certain requirements are met. The money comes from an entertainment tax levied on the customer at the box office, but it is untaxed income when the film companies get it. Naturally it is a strong temptation to "make a British film" (with a basically British crew and some British financing) when this means sharing in the box-office rebates provided by the Eady plan. Some of this money, too, is frozen, which of course means further involvement in foreign production.

There are many reasons for using foreign locations. The decision to shoot most of the picture abroad is not necessarily based entirely on blocked balances, subsidies, and the blandishments of Italian or British co-financiers.

The determining reason may often be an artistic one. The producer-director sometimes options a script on the assumption that it can only be shot in Israel or in Africa. The story demands it. The action could not be effectively developed against familiar American backgrounds, even if they "look like" the foreign locale.

Furthermore, the distant place may be just as important as the expensive star in building the "production value" that makes the picture sell. In fact, the star may already be overseas (seeking income tax advantages) or may want to take a trip overseas, and the two factors will reinforce each other.

Thus the artistic reason is inextricably mingled with the search for elements of audience appeal. The basic story may call for geographical splendor, but the publicity office may call for it even more strongly. Ever since *Three Coins in the Fountain* gave moviegoers their first CinemaScope tour of Rome, the foreign locale has been judged an "exploitable" factor. A producer-director, by the very tension of his hyphenation, has to think about commerce and aesthetics at the same time. When he thinks about the "values" of overseas location, he doesn't try too hard to distinguish between the demands of the story itself and the expectations of the big audience he hopes it will appeal to.

Furthermore, the American audience — so much more familiar with faraway places since World War II, so much more exposed to them by the wide screen — is now joined by an equally potent worldwide audience. Authenticity of background is a most important appeal in foreign lands. A story about Israel, filmed in Israel, may be of outstanding interest in Japan, and vice versa. Certainly it is hard to get away with a studio-produced picture about the Orient in the Oriental market.

None of these pressures can be altered much by the conscious resolve of individual producers to stay and work in Hollywood. Nor are they likely to be much affected by union resolutions, pickets, or boycotts. Hollywood labor-management meetings, however, have justifiably called attention to those "runaway" producers who try to save a few dollars by incorporating under a foreign flag — pretending to be foreign for tax purposes but claiming to be American for distribution advantages.

There will always be a Hollywood, technically speaking. The tradition is there, the laboratories are there, the skills are there. A great center of trained technicians draws business to itself, as the enormous volume of TV-film production attests. But there are also changing currents of comparative wage scales, import quotas, and national currency restrictions. There are broad shifts in audience interest, story sources, and directorial desires. There are some stars and directors who don't want to work in Hollywood any more, for reasons of their own. Sometimes they just don't want to have studio executives peering over their shoulders. If they can't have all the financial independence they want, at least they can have distance.

As for the labor costs of shooting in foreign countries, apparently the advantages and disadvantages tend to cancel out. Producers who have tried it say: "Yes, sometimes foreign crews can be smaller and cheaper than in Hollywood. But they may also work less efficiently, and sometimes they make costly mistakes."

The biggest labor advantage in foreign production is the availability and cheapness of extra players — onlookers, armies, and mobs. The cost of a first-rate revolution or massive battle is prohibitive in present-day Hollywood. The rise in the American standard of living has made spectacular films into foreign affairs.

Pleasing Everybody in the World

What does the world audience want? This is the big question for the theatrical film producer. If the domestic market is only half the box office, then the producer's judgment about a proposed script cannot be based only on his guesses about American audiences. His know-how must cover the whole world.

There is some form of censorship in nearly every country. The censoring agency has a great deal to say about what the audience will see. Conformity to the censor's standards is the first and most obvious step in getting a picture into a foreign theater.

Every major releasing company has a man in the foreign department whose primary duty is to study censorship practices abroad. He usually is located in Hollywood, where he can get a look at proposed story projects at an early stage and give his advice. If he feels that censors in several important countries will apply the scissors, his warning will be taken seriously. He may say: "The Japanese aren't so worried any more about implications of premarital sex relationships, but the Latin-American countries are still very touchy about it." Or he may demand that certain scenes of torture and violence be written out of the script because they are sure to be taken out of the film in India, Indonesia, and England. If he vetoes a script, the odds against its becoming a film are very great.

Hollywood has to watch overseas censorship far more carefully now than censorship in the U.S. The history of motion picture trade relations is checkered with bans and cuts and political protests. The foreign censor has always been thin-skinned and powerful. But his opinions get a lot more attention now that the foreign box office is so important.

The careless tendency in the 1920's and 1930's (as brought out in a study by Dorothy Jones for the Massachusetts Institute of Technology in 1955) was to conform only to American feelings and let the foreign scissors slice where they might. Oriental types, for example, were used mainly as mysterious villains or comedy relief. Censors might ban and newspapers protest, but to no avail. Now such easy stereotypes are increasingly rare. Feedback from film salesmen in the Orient has seen to that. In this respect, international good feeling has been considerably advanced by the democracy of the international box office.

In certain countries, the censor plays a positive role. Japan, for example, permits a few pictures to come in "over quota" each year if they are of especially good quality. West Germany has a unique system of encouraging "good" films. When a panel of judges decides that a short subject or a feature is socially important or even of highly original entertainment value, they grant the picture a tax reduction. This can be as much as 10 to 20 per cent. Such favorable notice may also give the picture a boost at the box office.

The actions of foreign censors — though ultimately unpredictable — are at least tangible, and they tend to follow a pattern in certain countries. Beyond such official actions, there is always the basic riddle of audience taste.

Here is where the foreign sales adviser, ill equipped as he is, must wade in and make sweeping decisions. Foreigners, he insists, are stoically resistant to drawing-room comedies dependent upon verbal humor. They find baseball incomprehensible. They are likely to be unmoved by stories that have narrowly "American" themes. Above all, they will be unable to understand the assumptions behind any regional or social "problems" presented from an American point of view.

These broad taboos are based on bitter experience with specific movies. There is no particular reason to dispute them. Yet such generalizations are subject to change when a successful film manages to challenge them.

Until recently, for example, it was widely accepted in Hollywood that overseas markets are practically immune to musicals of any kind. Yet a study was made for M-G-M by Ronald Carroll in 1950 which found that M-G-M's musicals were preferred over all other types of films in 23 countries representing 70 per cent of the foreign market. This new generalization, therefore, will last only until the surprising list of new musicals scheduled for 1962-63 turn out to be popular in Australia, Turkey, and Sweden simultaneously.

The Carroll study found out a remarkable fact, which still seems to be influencing production decisions. There was only one picture of the 126 M-G-M releases over a period of four years (September 1946 to August 1950) which brought in twice the average box office in every country in which it appeared. That picture was *The Three Musketeers.* The moral seemed clear: the world-wide audience wants adventure and spectacle. With the ponderous success overseas of such costume dramas as *Quo Vadis* and *The Ten Commandments,* the moral has hardened into a proverb. Action, pomp, and derring-do require no dubbing.

Even such a neutral corner as the Department of Commerce recognizes this trend. Nathan D. Golden, the department's respected motion picture analyst, wrote in the 1959 Film Daily Yearbook that business abroad could be expected to improve with the impending arrival of such "epic type" films as *Ben-Hur* and others.

Egypt has for years forbidden films to be shown that deal with Israel or with predominantly Jewish themes or characters. When *Ivanhoe* began to go into general release, M-G-M crossed Egypt off the list as a matter of course. But there was evidently something fascinating about the spectacle and adventure in this film. The Egyptian exhibitors wanted it. After the censor got through, according to Robert Vogel, M-G-M's foreign adviser, only half an hour of the picture was left. Nevertheless, *Ivanhoe* was very popular. Metro could put it down as the year's biggest box-office hit in Egypt.

Why should a producing company fret over a little picture which may not do well in certain countries when a big lavish picture will probably appeal to almost all countries? Why make a difficult film about contemporary American problems when one about antique heroes with no national identity will cause fewer problems at the box office?

It would be far more comfortable for the foreign departments staff if all they had to sell, year after year, were pictures like *Ben-Hur* and *The Ten Commandments*. How easy it would be if the world public wanted nothing else!

But in spite of censorship restrictions — and regardless of advice by conservative sales representatives overseas — many other kinds of stories find their way into foreign theaters. The appeal to the lowest common denominator of desire for sex and violence is a worldwide phenomenon.

The Melodramatic Image of America

The overseas box office is more and more a source of moral ambivalence for American film distributors. Even if it were possible to forecast what people want, is it right to give them what they want?

It is a proverb among film salesmen that people in small towns all over the world tend to enjoy the same films that go well in American small towns — that the big city audience, too, is the same at home or abroad. But are there sometimes compelling reasons of public policy for making a distinction? Should some films be sent overseas and others withheld? Does the American producer or distributor have a responsibility of choice?

This is a question of values, of course, and it applies to all communication at all times in history. It is broad in its implications. At the present time, it happens to be closely linked to patriotism and the cold war. Part of the controversy is whether American films properly "represent" American life, especially to the neutral or uncommitted nations.

The negative view was expressed with pertinency and passion by Norman Cousins in a *Saturday Review* editorial as long ago as January 21, 1950:

. . . the fact is that the movies do not accurately reflect America and Americans. We have more than our share of humanity's faults but we by no means monopolize them. Nor are we predominantly a nation of murderers, gangsters, idlers, deadbeats, dipsomaniacs, touts, tarts, and swindlers, as Hollywood would have us appear . . .

Some of us find something to do with our hands other than to drape them around long cocktail glasses, expensive cigarette holders or smoking revolvers. Some of us even read a book occasionally and find something to talk about other than a scheme to murder our wives or our business partners. And, while we like to hold our own in discussion or debate, it isn't true that the only rebuttal is a sock on the jaw.

There are various good answers to this kind of indictment. Eric Johnston replied immediately by calling attention to the many fine films Hollywood has released. He declared that most of the pictures which might be criticized "make no pretense of realism." He scoffed at the notion that foreign audiences think of America as a land of cattle rustlers and gangsters: "Of course they don't. No more than Americans believe all Italians steal bicycles because they saw the Italian picture, *Bicycle Thief*.

Samuel Goldwyn contributed to this exchange of views by defending the need of people everywhere for entertainment, not propaganda. He warned against the dangers of censorship and the distortions of "sweetness and light," for "as a free people, dare we hide from the world the ugly and show only the good? That would appear to be borrowing from the technique of totalitarians."

Another kind of defense involves supermarkets and factory parking lots. Though the story be cheap and its characters repugnant, at least the film may inadvertently show our high standard of living. A single gleaming kitchen may be attributed by an Iranian or Arabian to a set designer's dream, but a thousand cars are hard to fake. This argument assumes that our material advantages are our best ambassadors of good will.

Premier Sukarno of Indonesia, speaking in Hollywood

in 1956, supported this argument but at the same time hinted at what it might lead to: "In a world of inequality, you and your products cannot be non-controversial. You have helped to build up the sense of deprivation of man's birthright, and that sense of deprivation has played a large part in the national revolutions of post-war Asia."

The fact remains that for years there has been a constant stream of protests from India and Indonesia, from Viet Nam, the Middle East, Africa, and England, that American films seem to be characterized by violence and brutality. Can there be any doubt that many of the people who see these films believe that Americans, too, are characteristically violent and brutal — as well as rich? Over and over again, visitors to the U.S. are astonished to discover the familiar, peaceful facts of common life in this country.

Why should we expect foreign audiences, especially in areas of relative illiteracy, to be even more mature than we are? Can we honestly say that we, as moviegoers, are always very careful not to judge Italians — and especially Frenchmen — by the movies they send us?

The record at middle and lower levels of American movie making is too consistent to ignore. The image is forceful, warlike, bullying. During 1953, the major Hollywood distributors made available 174 films that could be described as having "American" themes. Of these, about half were either westerns or other melodramas of violence. Three years later, in 1956, there were 210 films on American themes, and the dramas of violence had risen to 59 per cent. Not all of these films were shown extensively overseas: the censors saw to that. But it is startling to realize that American film makers, from 50 to 60 per cent of the time, chose to show their country as a place of conflict and violence.

Westerns are habitually praised for their black-and-white moral values — the good man wins and the bad man dies. But the search for new twists of plot and characterization has turned all the characters gray. The criminal has become, by comparison, as attractive as anybody. What remains, in any case, is the constant appeal to fist and gun as the apparent way to settle disputes in America.

What about the younger generation overseas? American films appeal to them as much as they appeal to youth in America. We know that films helped to make rock-and-roll popular in Japan. Can we deny that American westerns and murder stories have given Japanese young people repeated images of excitement and crime? Can we deny that these may have inflated their basic postwar restlessness and rootlessness into mob action and unprecedented acts of violence? Any objective study of run-of-the-mill Japanese pictures since the war would reveal the frank imitation of American film models. The movies based on Shintaro Ishihara's stories are a case in point.

The apologists for the motion picture industry cannot claim, on the one hand, that American movies have spread the American way of life — from fashions in hats to democracy — and then deny, on the other hand, that

American movies could ever have contributed to juvenile delinquency overseas. They cannot have it both ways.

Even the so-called "quality films" from the U.S. are riddled with decadent themes of late. What do we expect foreign leaders to think of our family life when one of the "best" films of the year is *Cat on a Hot Tin Roof*? Why should we expect alertness and responsibility among the new generation in Africa when the model of American life they see at a downtown theater is a re-issue of *The Wild One* or *Blackboard Jungle*, with *Sweet Bird of Youth* one of the coming attractions?

The situation is bound to get worse before it gets better. The flow of television films to Europe, Japan, and South America has just begun. New developments in translation by voice dubbing have made it possible to sell a whole TV series in a foreign language.

So far, there has been a kind of balance between "action" series and light comedies. But the balance is bound to shift as more of the westerns and "private eye" shows come on the market from the current wave in this country. Latin-American countries, particularly, have been receptive to crime melodramas like "Highway Patrol," "Interpol Calling," "Jet Jackson, Flying Commando," "Mr. D.A.," "New Adventures of Martin Kane," "New York Confidential," "Sea Hunt," "Lockup."

Perhaps this is no surprise, in view of the historic prevalence of violent political change in Latin America. But it is a harsh note at a time when the cold war has suddenly come so close to our shores. In a hemisphere now dominated by the Cuban adventure in revolution, it is not pleasant to think that these weekly packages of violence may be North America's main cultural contribution to its Latin neighbors in the next few years.

Restriction or Responsibility?

"Drama is about extreme cases. Drama, from Sophocles to O'Neill, has seldom done a good public relations job for any country."

In these two sentences, Geoffrey Shurlock, administrator of Hollywood's Production Code, has summed up the fundamental problem underlying any ambassadorial function for American motion pictures.

Drama, most critics agree, is based upon conflict. The theatrical motion picture very often turns out to be simply conflict in motion. Film is essentially a physical medium, and it is not surprising that it turned, very early in its history, to the excitement of physical conflict. So long as conflict and shock are basic to drama — so long as twist endings and offbeat characterizations are interesting to audiences — these things will be more important to motion picture producers than precise truth or balanced reporting or even good will.

The question is not whether pictures like *On the Waterfront* or *The Defiant Ones* present a dramatized and therefore a distorted view of American problems. This is a question for students and critics of the film medium to debate — and it is worth debating, case by case. The art of the film has a long way to go in learning how to cope with public issues. But the question for public policy is whether, on balance, foreign audiences see an excessive number of American films with the easy plot lines of violence and passion. And if there are too many, what can be done about it?

Federal censorship or even federal "guidance" is not likely to offer any special advantages, and the dangers run deep. A Washington official is no better prepared than a film producer to make decisions, pro or con, on scripts or on markets. Even the most gentle advice leads to the most surprising results.

A disturbing example of experimental censorship is already before us. The U.S. Information Agency has exerted firm pressure on choices of film titles in four countries whose opinions are important to the U.S. — Turkey, Yugoslavia, Poland, and Viet Nam. Under an American invention called the Informational Media Guaranty program, the federal government provides dollar exchange services at a favorable rate in these four blocked-currency countries. In effect, the United States pays the distributor his film rental until the frozen foreign funds become available.

This is a most useful and interesting way of encouraging international communication. But for several years there was an approved list of titles. This list included only films tending to show the U.S. in a favorable light. Granted that the emphasis was placed on promoting "good" films — that is, "representative" ones — this was nevertheless clearly a case of censorship by the U.S. government of the films Yugoslavs, Poles, Turks, and Viet-Namese could see. It didn't even give them the opportunity to do their own censoring.

The producers most aggrieved by this USIA policy were the fly-by-night independents who thrive on crime and horror pictures. Nothing much was lost to civilization because these countries were not encouraged to see *Bottom of the Bottle, The Fly, Fort Massacre, Girls on the Loose, Guns, Girls, and Gangsters, Live Fast, Die Young, Love Me Tender,* or *Riot in Juvenile Hall.* But on the same 1958 list of films the USIA refused to help were *Anna Lucasta, Crime in the Streets, The Defiant Ones, A Hatful of Rain, I Want to Live, The Last Hurrah, No Down Payment, Paths of Glory, Pork Chop Hill,* and *Time Limit.* Most of these films were judged by various American critics to be among Hollywood's best.

It is true that a distributing company has the option of sending its picture into the country without benefit of the Media Guaranty program. But if this governmental "screening out" process were to be extended for a long period, or extended to other countries, it would unquestionably act as a brake on the making of certain kinds of films in this country — especially those films that call attention to evils in society.

In the era of the dominant foreign market, any kind of government pressure on world distribution, no matter how well intentioned, tends to have a marked effect on production. Censorship abroad can no longer be separated from censorship at home.

The pressures from censors, theater managers, and co-production financiers overseas to devitalize — indeed to de-Americanize — the common run of films from Hollywood studios grows greater all the time. For the federal government to add to those pressures would make our pictures so bland and diplomatic and characterless that no healthy American individualist could recognize his countrymen on the screen. Samuel Goldwyn is certainly right when he warns of the distortions of "sweetness and light."

If the federal government wants films made in such a way as to separate the domestic and the foreign market, the obvious answer is some kind of subsidy. Every major film-producing country provides such support, through a box-office rebate or some other means. But it is extremely difficult to invent a system of subsidy which avoids the censoring function. And a proposal for government subsidy with no reference to the content of films would seem meaningless to the congressmen who would have to vote on it.

The imposition of any effective system of restraints and values can come only through informal relationships within society itself. Restraints operate far more effectively when they are unofficial and integral to the social system. The important — and difficult — thing is for both Hollywood and American society to find new points of contact.

Film trends are usually begun by individual decisions, by the stubbornly creative individual film maker. They are supported and continued by social response. A society which wants more vitamins in its screen fare will encourage film producers to want to be better and wiser — more deeply aware of the tangle of world issues.

During the 1960's, Hollywood film makers will be forced to be aware of the feelings of audiences abroad. The effects on the content of films will inevitably vary with the individual producer's sense of responsibility and with the quality of his information and background about foreign feelings and needs. A man with a strong sense of obligation may be meticulous — in a negative way — about such things as censorship problems and the representation of national types on the screen. He may even search hopefully for stories that might add in a positive way to world understanding. A producer, on the other hand, who is careless of such obligations will seek the shekels and let the duty go. He will pitch his appeal to the lowest common response of everyman everywhere, and his vested interest will be to keep that response low, undemanding, and unchanging.

Responsibility is a slippery word, and it carries no binding guarantees. It implies that finding new and better things to pour into the channels of communication is the most satisfying policy — the way to stay in business and be respected by society.

The burden of responsibility must rest, in the last analysis, not on governmental restrictions, but on Hollywood producers themselves. They have the daily decisions to make. Cecil B. deMille put the situation forcefully in a speech to the Screen Producers Guild three years before he died:

When leaders of nations tell us — as the highest officials of Egypt and Burma have told us — that as boys they derived their conceptions of the world, their ideas of right and wrong, from American motion pictures, they bring home to us our awe-inspiring responsibility. It is a sobering thought that the decisions we make at our desks in Hollywood may intimately affect the lives of human beings, men, women, and children throughout the world.

The main thing theatrical film makers can do, having already begun to face the economic facts of the world market, is to admit to themselves that there are positive duties involved in reaching a world audience — that they have a colossal amount to learn about the real world at home and abroad — that instinct and imitation and inbreeding are not enough. It is not pleasant to keep remembering this, nor easy to know what to do about it. But those who do will have far better prospects of competing in the long run, because their awareness of the world will help them reach the world audience with messages that lift the heart and open the pocketbook too.

There is one fundamental way in which motion pictures can help to project a better understanding of America overseas. But this, to be well done, would require an approach to communication completely different from the usual Hollywood pattern.

If drama is about "extreme cases," documentary is about the familiar, the human, the usual, revealing the unseen wonders of the ordinary, the poetry of daily life. If drama uses plot and actors to achieve impact through conflict, the documentary may use actual people, locations, and events to achieve understanding. The theatrical experience, while it may have an educational effect, appeals primarily to that in man which is thrilled or strained or excited. The documentary experience, while it may also have an emotional effect, primarily appeals to that in man which judges, learns, and remembers.

During World War II, the Office of War Information had to become a film production agency. It had been decided that nonfiction films about American life were highly desirable for overseas use in order to balance some of the distorting excitements of American theatrical films. The nonfiction films that existed, however, were mostly unsuitable for foreign tastes. They were either dull "educationals" or "industrials" with a built-in sales pitch. The OWI had to go to the film makers — a few from Hollywood, most of them from the little companies in New York — to fill specific needs.

In recent years, quality documentaries about America have been few and far between. Tours of patriotic shrines, state chamber of commerce travelogues, and Presidential speeches are poor substitutes for international communication. Yet this is what the USIA has been forced to subsist on.

In Canada, the National Film Board, set up by John Grierson, survived the war to become the world's finest nonfiction film-producing organization. In Puerto Rico, a group of dedicated amateurs in the government's education program have made some of the most remarkable films in the history of documentary. The United States has felt no need for such a program, either in Washington or in Hollywood.

Some day American documentary film makers may have another chance, as they had during World War II. Even the Hollywood people who worked for the armed services were touched by the zeal of factual communication — Darryl Zanuck, George Stevens, Frank Capra, John Huston, and Garson Kanin for the Signal Corps, John Ford and Louis de Rochemont for the Navy, William Wyler for the Air Corps. Hollywood seems to have no affinity for such things now, nor any awareness of what to do if government proposals were forthcoming. The "documentary" as Hollywood sees it is a series like "Dragnet" or "Naked City," based on some shred of legal record and tailored to the plots that fit the theatrical tradition.

The nonfiction films that meet a national need are almost always made — whether in government, in industry, in the universities, in TV, or in the nontheatrical film companies — by those rare individuals who are involuntarily seers and prophets. If they do it as a speculative

project, because there is "a need for better understanding," they usually lose their shirts. It is still true that the
kind of factual films which fascinate foreign audiences
ordinarily do not get made unless government or founda-
tions provide basic financial help.

To picture the common life in America in all its range
and multiplicity requires a staggering combination of art,
journalism, and social science, as well as a knowledge of
the techniques of film making. In postwar television,
Edward R. Murrow has done more than any other man
to meet these hard demands. He has been primarily concerned with showing the world to Americans rather than
Americans to the world, but his way of working is a model
for any who would try. Now that he is head of the USIA,
he has the opportunity to shift his focus from harsh problems to daily achievements. But he will carry with him
a built-in concern for truth, for background, for the persuasive detail of common experience.

Four recent successes in projecting America abroad
are worth remembering. They offer historic clues for any
thoughtful communicator.

For the Brussels world fair, Willard Van Dyke and
Shirley Clarke produced a series of two-minute motion
picture "loops," continuously projected, which revealed
more about the simple, familiar facts of life in America
than any feature film in recent memory. They were gems
of plotless impressions, moments of fond recollection
about faces, feet, bridges, and sunsets.

For the Moscow fair, Charles Eames, designer and

film maker, set up an overhead panel of seven huge screens which challenged the eye for twelve busy minutes with 2200 still photographs of American homes, supermarkets, universities, parking lots, overpasses, skylines, crowds, picnics, children playing, people going to work, to the theater, and to church. The most stunning visual experience since the first Cinerama production, this experiment in multiple projection has vanished from the world scene, although it was proposed at one time to show it in India.

The USIA chose a different projection technique for India — Walt Disney's Circarama. Successfully used at Brussels and Moscow, this eleven-screen system surrounds the audience with images originally taken by an eleven-camera unit mounted on a car or airplane. A simple travelogue script calls attention to America's most famous cities and national parks — and also its typical factories and wheatfields, schools and villages.

The final section of *This Is Cinerama*, as proposed and supervised by Merian Cooper (who made *Grass* and *Chang* into documentary landmarks many years ago) was simply an airplane trip across America — an unforgettable experience. Many an old State Department hand can remember how that first Cinerama production emptied the Soviet pavilion at the Damascus fair. But the lame attempts by Louis de Rochemont and Lowell Thomas to get by with old-fashioned travelogue scripts have driven Cinerama into the arms of M-G-M. The search is on for fictional stories that will somehow be bigger and bolder and better than *Ben-Hur.*

The wide screen still offers a golden opportunity to display some of the geographical splendor of America and her endless search for a better way of life. The grandeur of great men and the wonders of nature are suited for such a setting. A poet could even show, on such a canvas, the mysterious links of freedom in the daily democratic life. But what poet is rich enough, or stubborn enough, to find the way to get it done?

6

THE END OF THE ASSEMBLY LINE

"Why don't we put some sprocket holes in the
press book and throw the picture away?"

Steve Broidy, president of Allied Artists

THE THEATRICAL motion picture producer is now
in a very special position.

He doesn't have to see to it that all the small-town
theaters have a new bill twice a week. He doesn't have
to fill a newspaper every day, a magazine every month,
or an hour on a TV network every week. Like a book
publisher or a play producer, the Hollywood film maker
can take his time, choose what he wants, start when he's
ready. He has, if he can only learn to accept it, a new and
responsible role in the communication system of his country. It is a more comfortable role than it used to be. He
can concentrate on one good thing at a time. He doesn't
have to be in a hurry any more.

The Overproduced Picture

The Hollywood producer's new position has been
forced on him by two historic circumstances.

In the first place, the anti-monopoly decisions by the courts (ranging over the period from 1940 to 1950) which resulted in the divorcement of theaters from production-distribution companies, also resulted in the abolition of block-booking. The theaters no longer had to take what they were offered, in large and sometimes unidentified packages. The distributors, on the other hand, because they no longer owned theaters, felt no financial obligation to provide a steady stream of "product." Thus Hollywood began to cut down on its schedule of pictures long before TV pulled the bottom out of the market and sent countless theaters into bankruptcy.

In the second place, Hollywood's slow acceptance of television, beginning with transcontinental TV in 1951, has meant that the new system of electronic distribution has taken over the mass production of cheaply made films. Often the frantically busy TV producer works just across the hall, or down the studio street, from the office of the theatrical producer. The latter can say to himself thankfully: "There, but for the grace of God, go I."

For the individual film producer the combined effect of theater divorcement and the rise of television has meant freedom from the tyranny of the assembly line. It is no longer necessary for a studio to make 52 pictures a year — or for Hollywood to distribute 500 or more. Individual films are prospering in long-run engagements, and box-office grosses are increasing. In 1951, American motion picture companies produced 391 features. By 1954, the number had declined to 253. In 1960, after an upturn to 300 in 1957, annual production was down to 154.

The theatrical motion picture today stands somewhere between the stage play and the television show. This is not merely a description of box-office status and audience size. It is also a key to its creative freedom. The old deadlines of mass production are lifted. A producer can choose the script he wants, wait for the right cast, and release when circumstances are most favorable.

But has he really accepted his freedom? Has he been emancipated from the assembly line only to be frozen into a frantic kind of slow motion?

The curious thing about the now unblocked producer is that his freedom has increased his tensions. His new artistic advantage — his reduced work load — carries with it a heavy economic strain. His concern has become more and more fixed on one picture at a time, and for a longer time. Instead of taking the opportunity between productions to breathe the air of the changing world outside of Hollywood, he closes the windows, calls in the writers, and sets to work to polish his next script some more. The result often is a kind of overproduction, which weighs down the whole film with constant changes and takes away the natural freshness and flow of ideas and images.

Part of this persistent preoccupation with the present task is a natural outcome of the kind of work he does, and its traditional intensity. It has always been true that nothing seems to matter to a film maker except his latest picture and the way his audience is going to respond to it. During preparation and shooting, it is almost impossible for him to discuss anything else. But this habitual state of mind, arising from the complexity of film making, has been made more obvious by the cutbacks in production. The typical Hollywood artist has few outside resources. He doesn't have anywhere to go except back to work—or to parties where work is the main topic of conversation.

The new varieties of independent production, of course, only add to the strain. The independent producer usually has to stand or fall by the success of his latest film. He sees the whole world through the window of that one enterprise.

A man like Samuel Goldwyn, the perennial independent, has usually limited himself to one or two pictures at a time, sometimes paying consecutively for a dozen scripts of a story before he was satisfied. But now that films are more "special" than ever before, Mr. Goldwyn declares he must spend four years on one motion picture—two years in preparation and production, two years in exploitation and distribution. This was one of the reasons for the tired look of *Porgy and Bess* when it finally appeared.

Spectacle films have always been carefully prepared and zealously overproduced. But now the hazards of the foreign market make it even more important to remove from these harmless extravaganzas any thorns that might annoy some segment of the world audience. The hesitations and revisions on *Ben-Hur* were only exceeded by the constant rewriting job on the remake of *Mutiny on the Bounty* — in this case to please the star.

Normally, a little more time to think about a picture should improve it. But there is a crucial point of diminishing returns, especially when the story itself needs simplicity and spontaneity. The saddest example of overproduction in recent times was George Stevens' production of *The Diary of Anne Frank*, in which a first-rate director somehow lost sight of the delicate tragedy of that spirited little girl in a welter of traditional Hollywood tactics: a worldwide search for a "new star," a sound-stage contraption to shake the whole cast with a representation of an air raid, and the introduction of even more cumbersome plot mechanics to shake the audience with suspense.

Overproduction is not irrational. Its purpose is to draw a big audience. The more elaborate the preparations for a picture the greater the "talk-about" — according to Sindlinger opinion tests — in the press, the fan magazines, and the women's clubs. The more ribbons a picture is tied up with, the more likely it is to draw people who don't usually go to the movies — that extra audience which brings in extra profits. But the kind of ribbons that attract attention are getting more expensive all the time.

Overproduction is also an attempt to catch the salesman's eye. He has to be persuaded, long before the release date, that the producer's year-long effort will amount to a special event in the theaters. Whether the salesman is an independent himself or an employee of a major company, he is attuned primarily to money as a standard of judgment. If the production budget is big (he reasons) the exploitation budget has to be big enough to fit. If the production is planned from the beginning as a financial blockbuster, then it has to have special plans for release.

In the major metropolitan centers, the idea of a pre-release long run is increasingly accepted by distributors and exhibitors for the big spectacles and costly star-studded stories. But such farsighted faith in the "product" is seldom bestowed on the good little film which deserves a wider audience than a quick week in town will bring it. It is a historic irony that the salesmen — and also the top executives — had no faith whatever in *Lili* and grave doubts about *Marty*. Sure pictures are not as big as a house. They are only rare, like diamonds.

One way of setting budgets at blockbuster levels, right from the beginning, is to buy recent best sellers and hit plays. This pleases the salesmen because sometimes the high purchase price is itself a publicity point. And of course a "pre-sold" product is much easier to sell.

Original screenplays are not a totally lost art in Hollywood. The statistics usually look good on an annual basis. But it turns out that most of the originals are small-budget westerns, horror pictures, or science fiction films. A major picture like *The Apartment*, based on a script by Billy Wilder and I. A. L. Diamond, is a rarity indeed.

Top budgets are reserved for unoriginal films. The

salesmen assume they are easier to sell. The producers, in turn, assume that the salesmen will give these used plots (which cost so much money to buy in the first place) a top priority in publicity and advertising. There is no particular conviction anywhere along the line that the film medium has anything unique to offer. The purpose of the film is to re-enact the play, reshuffle the novel. The purpose of Hollywood is to be a used plot lot.

The Gray Flannel Men and the Decline of Style

Colossalism is a familiar nostrum in show business. Once more it is becoming a substitute for the vitamins of story sense and film sense. This is partly because of a slow, historic change in Hollywood's leadership.

The era of the hard-fisted, colorful pioneers is past. They lived and worked for an extraordinarily long span of time, but Cecil B. deMille, Jesse Lasky, Louis B. Mayer, Harry Cohn, and Joseph Schenck are gone. Everywhere the producers — whether independent, semi-independent, or staff — are beginning to have a gray-flannel look. Even the actors are sweating over taxes and account books.

The daring, irascible bosses of Hollywood's first fifty years had the excitement of show business in their veins. They gauged public taste in their own instinctive ways, having been only recently part of the public themselves. They may not have had much formal education, but for that very reason they were in tune with the audience of their time.

To a great extent, today's producer has grown up in the Hollywood scheme of things, under the shadow of the first, flashy entrepreneurs. Whether or not he is "second generation" by blood, he is at least the protected heir of an older order. He may know his way around the studios, and he may know all about the supposed special interests in the hard-core movie audience. He is likely to have a more educated alertness to the opinions of educated men. But he may be efficient without being effective — a calm, well-informed coordinator, making films without passion and without distinction. His formula, if he has any, is to remake old successes and spend a lot more money on them. What was box office for the older generation should be box office again, if it's modernized, with the right trimmings added. The used plot is even better if it has already been made, once or twice before, into a successful movie.

This formula usually requires little explanation to New York bosses and bankers. Bigness goes over big in traditional financial circles. Bankers can only respond with blank stares and long silences to the earnest plea: "It's a great story! It's different!" Investment money goes for "star values" and "production values."

A new generation of film makers, torn between the vivid remembrance of their swashbuckling predecessors and the sober actuality of accountants, bankers, and salesmen, finds it hard to insist upon the new and untried, either in stories or in techniques. The result is a widespread lack of pride in the film medium — in film as film and the things it can uniquely accomplish.

Outside of Hollywood, cinematic ingenuity seems to grow and flourish. The world has been pleased and astonished by a few quick cuts in *Hiroshima, Mon Amour* which bring the past suddenly in view — by a dizzy camera movement in *The Cranes Are Flying* which suggests death in battle — by the shadowy, unexpected introspections of *Wild Strawberries* — by the almost palpable color in *Gate of Hell* — by the close observation of family life in *Pather Panchali* — by the brilliant directorial authority of *La Dolce Vita* — by the confident buildup to a final slapstick scene in the Peter Sellers comedies — by the peculiar insouciance of objects and gadgets in *My Uncle*.

Why should the film makers of France, Russia, Sweden, Japan, India, Italy, and England monopolize the praise of critics and the attention of much of the public? Why should foreign films be carrying on the heritage of America's D. W. Griffith in extending the resources of film in new-old ways?

The vice of the assembly line system was its tendency to spin off so many cheap films that were so poor from a critical standpoint. The vice of the post-television system of "fewer and better" pictures is its tendency to magnify to such a degree the importance of expensive films. If *Ben-Hur* had failed, M-G-M would have gone bankrupt. If *Spartacus* had failed, Universal would have been in a very shaky condition. The budget of *Cleopatra* carried with it the fate of Twentieth Century–Fox.

"Fewer and better" is more of an incantation than a fruitful policy. What Hollywood really loves to do is to make pictures bigger. When the chance came to make fewer pictures, it was inevitable that some of them would get bigger, more expensive, more overloaded with "production values," and the public went along. Ever since the 8-reel *Quo Vadis* was first imported from Italy in 1913, it has been clear that the public enjoys bigness.

With high stakes, of course, there is more margin for profit. Why labor to bring forth a nice little $500,000 picture on the chance that an advertising and distribution budget of $800,000 will bring in a net of $300,000? Why gamble on a reasonable return when you can just as easily wait around for a couple of top-ranking stars and a best-selling book — and then gamble on a $2,000,000 profit instead?

Colossalism is supposed to keep the community prosperous, too. In many ways, despite the everpresence of upheaval and change, Hollywood has become a conservative, settled town. Every major guild now has a new building of its own. The International Alliance of Theatrical and Stage Employees has won power and position since the jurisdictional strikes of the late forties. Contracts are ever fatter and more favorable to individual workers. Pictures have to be expensive to keep both the workers and the stars in the style to which they have become accustomed.

Yet costliness and the rigidity of guild and union rules have begun to drive creative people away. "Runaway" production is partly the result of restless, independent, creative people trying to get away from Hollywood's overpowering budgets. Foreign locations may be costly, too, but the controls are often looser and the chances greater for the kind of filmic excitement that artistry alone can achieve.

The art of the film has fallen by the wayside in Hollywood. There seems to be less and less opportunity for the passion and persistence of young people willing to make pictures for small stakes. Often the youngest people don't have as much taste or ability as they think they have. But they may have freshness and style and surprise. New young directors might make the mistake of underproducing a picture now and then. Inevitably they will waste money somewhere along the line. But out of the $20,000,000 invested in *Mutiny on the Bounty*, fifty lowbudget films could have been made. Who is to say which proposition is more wasteful?

One of the best answers for the runaway production problem is low-budget production here at home. When Val Lewton and Orson Welles had a free hand for a while at RKO in the 1940's, they trained two young film editors who have turned out to be leading directors today. These two men, Mark Robson and Robert Wise, have kept a lot of people busy and well paid in the 1950's. They learned their trade and developed their art by making "little pictures."

Bigness isn't everything, and its appeal doesn't last forever. Bigger doesn't necessarily mean better, any more than fewness guarantees goodness. Quality is not achieved by subtracting from the total number of productions and multiplying the number and cost of people and things in the remaining productions on the list. Quality has nothing to do with either multiplication or magnification. It is something that sneaks into a film as a reflection of somebody's quality of mind and heart. It comes from the long-range commitments of specific human beings.

The men behind the screen, the men with the power to decide, may never feel secure enough to insist upon art. But they need not be so short-sighted as to squeeze out of American films all uniqueness and sense of style. The ones who love the medium most are the ones who work with it most intimately — the writers and directors who have to make the story come to life on the screen. If Hollywood is to come alive again, the men with the power to do so must find and cherish a group of writers who can develop stories directly for the screen and a group of directors who want more than anything else to use the unique resources of camera, editing, and sound.

Then it will be possible to have more "faith in the product" because there will be, in the first instance, faith in the creative art of the film.

CAN HOLLYWOOD HELP ITSELF?

"Did you hear about the producer who was such a snob he wanted an unlisted Social Security number?"

Item in a Hollywood column

THE FOUR expanded freedoms that have come in the wake of the television revolution are not sharp breaks with the past. They have developed naturally — and rather blindly — out of older, earlier tendencies, in response to competitive commercial pressures. They have taken little account of social needs, and it is not surprising that they are subject to mounting criticism.

Four Freedoms — and Three Limitations

The move toward so-called "adult" films simply revives the traditional tendency to define sex as that subject which has the widest appeal. The frantic search for the lowest common appeal has occurred before, especially at moments of economic crisis. Such "freedom" has always gone too far and has stirred public criticism by parent and church groups. This time, both dialogue and dramatic situations have become more extreme than anybody thought possible at the outset, and the criticism has become equally blunt. The next step is to accept classification of films as the logical result of the "adult" film trend.

The move toward independent production follows the lines of the old United Artists relationship with the actors who formed the company. It has gone a great deal farther this time. The freedom of independence has diffused responsibility as well as costs. It seems to encourage individuality and creativity but actually re-enforces, through isolation and fear, the appeal to the lowest common denominators of sex and violence. Therefore criticism of the "sameness" of Hollywood product continues unabated. The next step is to encourage experimentation and new ideas within companies big enough to risk the variety of a balanced program.

The move toward overseas distribution is simply an expansion of activity that began when films were first made. American films have always gone abroad in search of the biggest possible market. That the overseas market is now greater than the American market — and the audience three times larger — means a greater freedom to serve foreign tastes. But it also means less likelihood that "problem films" about American life will be produced at all. The failure of Hollywood to tell this side of the story of America to Americans and to tell the good side of America abroad will continue to be criticized, until film makers take the next step and reach out for a more fundamental acquaintanceship with America and the world, starting, perhaps, with a willingness to undertake nonfiction subjects.

The move toward fewer and bigger productions is an old instinct in show business and is hardly new in Hollywood. But freedom from the artistic tyranny of the assembly line has provided a real opportunity for maturity — more time to think, to concentrate on quality. This challenging opportunity is still mired in traditional colossalism and the overproduction of one picture at a time. The narrow vision of Hollywood's gray-flannel second generation will continue to be a target for criticism, here and abroad, until new commitments to quality make room for the original screenwriting and directorial brilliance that can re-establish an American style in cinema.

Hollywood is always under criticism, and always responds to it with surprise and an air of injured pride. But Hollywood's position in the world is changing. Neither criticism nor impassioned defense can deflect that change very much. With new freedoms come new responsibilities. The question is whether the response to change and to criticism will be in any degree far-seeing. The question is whether the 1950's will be remembered as the decade of strong new freedoms or simply as the decade of Hollywood's gradual, uncontrollable disintegration.

There are some, outside of Hollywood, who predict that the system is irreversibly on the way into a ditch of dullness. The only salvation of the moving image, they say, is to move to New York, get support from separate investors in the manner of the Broadway theater, and do the inexpensive, offbeat pictures which will really reflect the malaise of our times.

There are some in Hollywood who insist, on the contrary, that the more things change the more they will remain the same. They draw their tattered cloaks about them and look for still another "sexy property" that will enable them to drift a while longer in the mental atmosphere of Palm Springs and Las Vegas.

But neither the left-wing experimentalist nor the right-wing sensationalist is necessarily in touch with the core of American life. Neither takes account of the traditional relationship between the American film maker and his audience. Entertainment for the whole family is still a profitable and useful purpose for Hollywood. If the shaky, dispersed institution that is Hollywood can re-establish contact with the people, then its survival, year by year, will become surer and prouder.

There are plenty of roadblocks that can keep Hollywood from moving ahead in any continuing, self-assured role.

There are other industry problems — the racking conflicts which sometimes occur on boards of directors and which nearly destroyed M-G-M and Twentieth Century–Fox — the frequent dominance in Hollywood of the publicity-powered personality who can talk his way into a position of authority but cannot win the confidence of truly talented people — the rigid loyalty to old-fashioned commercialism in advertising — the almost psychopathic resistance to critical reviews that are really critical.

There are other external problems — the tendency of the Un-American Activities Committee and similar government inquiries to scare producers and writers away from significant subjects — the buzz-saw complaints of small but organized pressure groups — the broader Puritan heritage in this country which insists that drama is inherently destructive to morale — the dilemma of "cultural exchange" *vs.* ideological competition with Russia.

These are older, more familiar troubles. They will continue to make life more or less miserable for artists, craftsmen, critics, and the audience. They are aspects of the environment over which Hollywood's film makers have very little control.

In the background, however, are three fundamental limitations which tend to keep the theatrical film industry from achieving any kind of institutional maturity as a part of the American scene. They are self-imposed limitations. They represent simple neglect — of the past, the present, and the future. Over the years, the motion picture industry has failed to appreciate the history of its art or develop new channels for its talent, and there has been no consistent effort to keep in touch with the daily life of Americans.

Many of the people who make movies are strongly self-centered and excessively stubborn. They have to be. No other profession requires quite the same extraordinary combination of knowledge and instinct, delicacy and force, patience and impatience. But the best of them are keen and intelligent men, quick to grasp the dimensions of a problem, eager to put ideas into concrete form. They are restless manipulators sometimes, but that's their business. They have to be able to plan and control the most complex kind of communicative art man has ever devised; they have to be masters of technology, human relations, and art.

Perhaps it is too much to expect such a scattered, directionless group of people — often jealous, constantly quarreling — to undertake more than I have already asked: a reassessment of attitudes and an awareness of new freedoms and responsibilities. But I think the men and women who manage the marvelous feats of movie making would not be interested in a challenge that was muted or incomplete.

Don't Look Back!

Hollywood is no citadel of modesty. But the things to be proud of always seem to be the things of the moment — a new glamour queen, a new wide-screen process, a new box-office record, a new adventure in location shooting in some far-off place. This preoccupation means that most of the key people in Hollywood don't seem to be concerned with either the past or the future.

The motion picture industry has little interest in its own history. Unlike the oil, steel, or automobile companies, the film distributors are completely uninterested in early equipment or historic models as mementos of a great tradition. Last year's movies, far from having any trade-in value, are dangerous competition for audience attention. This week's releases are the ones that the businessmen are interested in.

The re-release market? *Gone With the Wind,* to be sure, is a perennial moneymaker, and *The Wizard of Oz* is a special annual sale to television. There are certain double bills that make out fairly well when some highly touted release unexpectedly plays to empty houses. But in general, old films have only one future, and this is a recent discovery — TV. After television is done with them, the old prints will go to the graveyard.

When the first blocks of Hollywood features were sold to TV, the contracts were astonishing. Sometimes everything was sold along with the rights — the negative, the prints, even the still photographs. The companies seemed to be overjoyed to get rid of the old junk that had been cluttering up their film vaults for so many years. Now the situation is chaotic. The films are more accessible, for a time, than they used to be. You can catch them on the "tube," over and over again — with cuts, of course, to fit the time and the commercials. Many are available through 16-millimeter distributors till the prints wear out. But ownership of the negatives is scattered among a hundred agents and corporations. Some of the old RKO and United Artists negatives have probably disappeared already.

There is no such thing as a general library of American feature films in this country. The Library of Congress catalogues them and theoretically has the right to demand a print, but has no place to store them. The Academy of Motion Picture Arts and Sciences has a right to demand any Oscar-winning film to show, but the Academy has no place to store them either. The Museum of Modern Art in New York has purchased a few "classics" from time to time, especially silent films, and a number of Hollywood sound productions were deposited there in the 1930's and '40's, but many of them were withdrawn when the rights were sold to television. Eastman House in Rochester, N.Y., is quietly seeking historic items, but is making no attempt to do a complete job.

Andrew Carnegie took it upon himself to see to it that printed books were bought, kept, and made easily available for a growing America in the nineteenth century. No comparable ideal of preservation, availability, and study has ever shaken the twentieth century world of motion pictures. There is a vague commercial notion that the jerky likeness of McKinley or Wilson in a newsreel may be worth preserving because of re-use payments in TV documentaries. But nobody, for the last sixty years, has been paying continuous attention to preserving the motion picture as a work of art.

From time to time, people on the periphery of power in Hollywood have proposed a museum. It would collect old costumes, old kinetoscopes, old scrapbooks, and perhaps, if the studios allowed, a few old films. Time after time, the proposal has failed to get sufficient backing.

Even now, with a Los Angeles County Motion Picture and Television Museum very nearly a reality, the physical

availability of films is a moot point for a wide range of titles. Down through the years, thousands of priceless pictures have been allowed to disintegrate, especially those
of companies no longer in existence. A few survive, in the
cellars and attics of private individuals who, by wisdom
or luck, chose to preserve them. These are now being
sought for the museum archives.

The prestige of the group promoting the new museum,
under the leadership of Sol Lesser, is extremely high.
There is every reason to suppose that it will tread successfully the narrow, compromise path between an educational institution and Disneyland. The movie companies
have evidently agreed to shoot some segments of their
productions on the museum premises (under controlled
sound conditions), in order to provide a good show for
tourists and good public relations for the industry. But
this concession appears to be the chief contribution of the
studios. The county government has had to provide much
of the basic financing, and the rest must come from paid
admissions. The notion that the film companies might
underwrite any merely historical landmark has never, in
the whole process of discussion and planning, been considered as a possibility. And whether there will be in the
film archives more than a few representative titles for each
year is yet to be determined.

The lack of interest in history extends, for the most part,
to written records as well. Cecil B. deMille was always
conscious of his role: his autobiography attests his meticulous record-keeping. Adolph Zukor has written a breezy

summary of his recollections, and many a star has collaborated on a life story. But the first serious history of a major studio was Bosley Crowther's *The Lion's Share*, published in 1957. And historians of the art of the film — Lewis Jacobs, Paul Rotha, Richard Griffith, Arthur Knight — have had little or no encouragement from American film companies.

Without building on its past, how can a major art industry grow? Many individuals try to keep alive their own old memories. The Screen Directors or Writers Guild occasionally starts up a special film series, and the Academy, for a while, used to run old Oscar winners, year by year. Such evenings of entertainment can lead to nostalgia — or sometimes to sincere imitation. They do little to build either a tradition or the kind of comparative criticism which might be creative.

There is no place for the study of film history in the Hollywood scheme of things. A producer can get a picture out of the vault to check on some supporting actor's performance for a casting decision. But the study of film, as film, is not part of the training — for producers, directors, writers, or anybody else. This is partly because there is no such thing as training.

The Closed Front Door

The industry has small concern for any long-term future. There are no official channels for developing new talent at any of the three main levels of need. In the search for "new faces" among performers, the movie companies make only sporadic attempts to develop their own. Unlike the electronics and aircraft industries in the nearby Los Angeles area, the major motion picture studios make little or no effort to seek out promising college graduates for training at the executive level. And entrance to the unions is almost completely closed except for occasional relatives and friends.

The popular phrase, "breaking into the movies," is a quite accurate statement of the way it's done. Even the most beautiful girl in the world, assuming she has been able to win a beauty contest and has also won some acting experience in a little theater or on TV, must have the help of a talent agent. Talent agents are busy people — very busy. Winning the attention of even a low-grade agent is not easy, and sometimes involves methods that have little to do with talent. After that, the task is to win the attention of a director or producer at just the time he is searching for a new face for a minor part in a new picture.

Since there are about five hundred others trying for the same thing, the attention-getting process is likely to succeed as much by accident or sheer persistence or an artful campaign in the trade papers as by a rational presentation of talent. The odds are all in favor of the brash, tough young thing who can keep on fighting for attention indefinitely. For every modest Eva Marie Saint who can survive this kind of "system" (and she did it in the far more rational atmosphere of early live TV in New York), there are a dozen Jayne Mansfields. A truly exotic talent, a deep personality, a sensitive Greta Garbo, is seldom found by turning in an order to the flesh merchants.

A rational industry-wide system of training talent is improbable, of course, even at the little theater level, for this would mean sharing secret information, inflating prices, and perhaps losing a star. Even the conscientious producer keeps under his hat his mental card file of ripening personalities. If he so much as praises or encourages an unattached youngster, this tends to attract competitive bids for her services. The old way and the safest way was the studio contract performer, on call at any time for a role in a current production, and in training the rest of the time with a studio dialogue coach. Under such circumstances, the ripening goes on in a more or less steady fashion — with disappointments and explosions, to be sure — but with some degree of security for both performer and producer.

Obviously nobody can plan a star. Even such qualified planners as Samuel Goldwyn and George Stevens have found this out to their sorrow. Heavily organized and publicized attempts to develop studio training groups or "stars of the future" have not lasted long. Nobody can say whether the next leading woman will turn up in a soda fountain or in Sweden. Nevertheless, assuming that the movies will always need both "personalities" and actors, it is still necessary to find them and develop them. Too many of the "big names" have lately left the scene forever.

Survival of the fittest may seem a logical theory for the

Hollywood jungle, but in show business as in life the whole environment becomes more civilized when someone decides to do a little planning. A systemless system which does no seeking — which depends on whatever the theater, the agents, and TV turn up — deserves what it gets: a rather high percentage of vultures, tigresses, and snakes.

The same is true of executive talent. If nobody is paying any attention to the future of the organization, it will probably fall into the hands of second-rate men. Friends, relatives, accountants, and lawyers can provide a comfortable environment for a dynamic and creative leader, but after he is gone such people are not likely to become creative overnight. The problem in Hollywood is different from the usual one of perpetuating the corporation. Personality judgments and psychological tests are shaky enough as predictions of leadership in the cool, steady conformity of a bank or an insurance company. Such tests are hopelessly misleading in the volatile atmosphere of a theatrical film studio. Yet the organization needs some way of protecting itself, in a time of crisis, against the ambition of every loudmouth who thinks he is another Thalberg. The most effective and creative producers in Hollywood are loath to undertake executive positions in the present disjointed state of the business.

There is no easy answer, and it would be wishful thinking to offer one. What is needed is simply a more open attitude — and a budget to support it. Jerry Wald has managed to get two or three "bright young men" assigned to his staff from time to time, despite the grim opposition of studio accountants. Max Youngstein was in a position, as vice-president of United Artists, to bring in a few promising people at the junior executive level. Yet the trend is still otherwise. The easiest way always seems to be a process of massive neglect, based on seniority, familiarity, and nepotism. In an industry so constantly shaken with change, it feels good to keep old, familiar faces around the executive luncheon table.

At the technical level, the resistance to new faces is overwhelming. Most Americans are aware of the protective systems of seniority worked out by labor unions in various basic industries. But the insecurity of Hollywood redoubles the yearning for steady employment. The routines get more deadly all the time. Top directors may be able to choose the top cameramen and other union people on a preference basis, if they are available, at salaries in keeping with their years of service. But the selection is limited to members of the unions.

A Hollywood studio is not permitted, under the terms of union contracts, to go outside the ranks for a young cameraman of talent. Union members must be used first. If all of them happen to be busy, the producing company may be able to get a promising young man of its own choice temporarily certified. Talented or not, this new man represents a breach in the theory of a fixed reservoir of talent, and it may be even harder for him to find a job the next time.

Film editors, set designers, script clerks, sound men, assistant directors, and a dozen other unions and guilds follow the same general pattern. "It was tough for me to get in," says the insider. "Why should I make it any easier for someone else?" There is no provision for union qualification through college training. The first essential for membership is to get a job; yet no one in the industry will hire a man unless he is already a member of the union. It looks like a hopeless merry-go-round, and it is.

There is only one sure way to get into the union. If the aspiring film technician has managed to be born in a motion picture family, he can expect friendly consideration, especially if his father or his uncle is already a member of the union he aspires to. There are tests, and the usual requirement of a definite job. But for the son of a cameraman or the nephew of an assistant director, the way in is easy. He is considered a fine addition to the reservoir of talent—perhaps the more so because he often brings to it little in the way of competitive ability.

The scandal of this way of doing things is doubly debilitating. It not only is fundamentally unfair and therefore destructive to morale in the industry. It also leads inevitably — as it usually does in any walk of life — to the decline of inventiveness and the atrophy of art. When the cards are stacked and the rolls are padded, talent gets left behind.

In general, the motion picture business is a closed system. It is not too difficult to move in sideways from a successful career in some other medium, as Elia Kazan came from the stage and Delbert Mann and others have come in from television. But the solidifying of union barriers has made it progressively harder for young people to rise vertically through the ranks. John Ford could begin as a stunt man in the silent days, Delmer Daves as a prop man, George Seaton and Billy Wilder as writers, Robert Wise and Mark Robson as editors, George Stevens as a cameraman, Alfred Hitchcock as a designer. But to move nowadays from one technical category to another is increasingly difficult. Even to move from camera assistant to camera operator takes a specified number of years, and it is practically impossible to move from the New York branch to the Hollywood branch of the same union.

One of the saddest changes of all is the disappearance from the Hollywood scene of the studio short subjects department. After the era of the silent comedy, the "short" was the only way for a new man to try out his own ideas without endangering a million dollars of somebody's feature budget. Fred Zinnemann and George Pal made their earliest mistakes and their first tentative triumphs within the small scope of the two-reelers. The grim meat grinders of TV film making have no time for tryouts and no interest in the expression of individuality. If Hollywood really wanted to develop new directing and production talent, the revival of the short subject would be the next thing on the schedule.

The motion picture industry always profits, directly and indirectly, when new creative talent comes into it. The inventive cameraman or cutter is potentially a new director, and every new director represents a chance for the art of the film to win new respect and support from the public.

The very nature of film as a complex, unstable art form calls for the utmost flexibility in the selection of its creative components. The daily drama of selection and promotion should have a variety of exits and entrances. The back door of nepotism and favoritism need not be the only open door. If the theatrical guilds, unions, and studios ever bring themselves to agree to grant a union card to one or two people each year from the universities which offer degrees in motion picture production, this would be an honorable and orderly way of opening the front door. University graduates who have already made several short films of their own are good risks for permanent employment. The blood line is a poor test of future usefulness. The thirteen American colonies made a big issue of that back in 1776.

Secondhand Seeing

Film fulfills its most valuable function, from a social point of view, when it illuminates contemporary experience. Yet this kind of concern for the present is quite different from a feverish preoccupation with the budget, cast, and schedule of a film. It calls for a wide-ranging awareness of the background and present tendencies in American life.

It is an old Hollywood axiom that "there is nothing wrong with the picture business that can't be cured by a good story." To this has now been added the necessity of producing "fewer and better pictures." The search for stories, certainly, is the main thing. The only trouble is that the search still seems to be carried on, for the most part, in the vague hope that something will turn up. The producer depends on agents, story editors, play producers, and novelists to supply him with his inspirations. With rare exceptions, the producer does not consider it his role to find new writers, to stir up new stories, or to find out firsthand the state of the world.

How can the film maker meet the needs of the public unless he knows the public's problems? How can he judge the stories on his desk unless he is acquainted with the temper of the times?

The Hollywood dilemma is the same as it always was: how to develop stories that are new and different and yet not so "far out" as to make the audience feel insecure — how to feed the sense of excitement and the sense of familiarity at the same time. The sense of excitement has been sought in these latter days by pointing the finger of shame at everybody — examining ingrown selfishness and sin over and over again, as if they were predominant aspects of the human condition. The illusion of security, on the other hand, has been sought by avoiding any really close contact with human life and sidestepping criticism of any specific segment of society. The people in these films are often not really recognizable, or even individual. Their sins are supposed to belong to all of us, therefore nobody in particular can complain. It is a dreary round of characters we meet on the screen these days, unclassifiable except as middle class, unidentifiable except by degrees of villainy or sloth. Humanity is affronted by these extremes, but who speaks for humanity?

The men who decide what stories to buy have lost touch with the daily concerns of mankind. They are certainly out of touch with the wider range of working people — with the miner who no longer works because of automation, with the supermarket manager who seldom meets his customers, with the government housing administrator who is helping integration work. They get their scripts from the same authors, agents, and playwrights who provide expense-account executives with a "shock" play on Broadway and their wives with a "shocking" novel at home. Such limited cultural cross-fertilization is not likely to be brilliantly fruitful in story ideas for the screen. The tired plots come from the old staple fantasies of sex and violence — and from show business itself.

One remedy for this paralysis of isolation is for Hollywood producers, directors, and writers to get out and look at the world — get acquainted with the present that lies all around them. If the Hollywood film maker is to gain and hold attention in the sixties, he must establish a new relationship with the people, new ways of access to their minds and hearts. The old familiar short cuts through the offices of publishers, play producers, and agents are getting to be dead-end alleys. The people are out there, waiting to be known.

Certain film makers today, unlike the studio-bound "supervisors" of yesteryear, seem more than willing to undertake new, refreshing experiences. They roam the world restlessly, as if they were shaking secrets out of far corners. Sam Spiegel, producer of *The Bridge on the River Kwai* and *Lawrence of Arabia,* is particularly fond of subjects that take him far afield; he scoffs at the limited outlook of Hollywood stay-at-homes. John Huston, now a producer-director, hasn't called Hollywood home for nearly ten years.

The typical foreign venture, however, tends to average out poorly as education. The director or producer finds that the business of making the film absorbs almost all of his energy. He gets to know the man he rents a location from, he talks a little bit on the sidelines with extra players, he hobnobs with local bigwigs who want to invite the star to dinner. But his basic, continuing relationships are with people in show business. He probably stays in a famous hotel patronized by stage and screen people. If he does any sightseeing after the shooting is finished, he will probably do it in the company of friends who will thoroughly insulate him from any close contact with the countryside and its way of life.

Even on location trips within the United States, only the most alert and unusual producer-director will take notice of incidental Americana. Otto Preminger may have turned up some roots of American politics while making *Anatomy of a Murder* in Michigan, and these may have helped him when it came to adapting *Advise and Consent* for the screen. Elia Kazan may have discovered a good deal more than characters for bit parts when he took his crew to TVA country for *Wild River*. But for the most part, preliminary location scouting is completely taken up with the specific purposes of the picture, and when production time comes, the pressures of daily costs are too great to allow any nonsense about local color.

What if certain key film makers in Hollywood were given the occasion and the opportunity, between pictures, to get completely away from show business for a while? What if they were given a real chance to get acquainted with American life? They have the time to do it — the new changes in Hollywood have seen to that. Would they have the inclination?

It is a radical thought, and yet not without precedents. The "sabbatical year" is familiar in universities. The recent trend toward liberal arts courses for busy executives indicates a yearning for broader-based experience as a background for decision making. The Nieman Fellowships at Harvard have long applied the notion to working journalists. Jean Renoir spent a term at the University of California at Berkeley, lecturing about films and talking with faculty and students.

Creative people, like scientists, can profit from a period of "basic research." The salutary effects would extend far beyond what the eye can see. It would open up whole new vistas of purpose and content for film making.

One logical base for basic research is a university — preferably one some distance from either New York or Los

Angeles. A university, far from being an ivory tower, is a community of scholars in search of truth, a busy center of information about all aspects of human life — past, present, and future. It is also, at its best, enormously alive: a place of youth and vigor and clashing opinions. The Hollywood producer who wishes to understand his changing public can find a very large segment of it among the youth on college campuses. More and more young people from all walks of life are enrolled in colleges every year, and the high school boys and girls waiting to get in are more and more oriented toward the values of higher education.

The university, too, could learn a few things from such a domestic Fulbright plan. Besides contributing, perhaps rather stiffly, to the further education of people in the movie industry, the professors and deans might also approach with curiosity and concern the phenomenon of mass entertainment as in fact a primary source of education in our time. The Hollywood visitor could function both as a graduate student and as a communicator — ready to listen and learn about city planning, southeast Asia, the history of education, or American literature, but also ready to talk to an appreciative audience about motion pictures.

Whatever the means may be, the problem is to combat Hollywood's traditional and continuing isolation from the common life in America. A momentary publicity junket into the hinterland with a newly released film is not enough. The need is to make a special effort — to take advantage of the traditional insecurity of hurry-and-wait. Scattered through the roster of producers, directors, writers, and actors are men and women who would welcome and could profit from an extended period of reacquaintance with the daily actualities of American life.

During World War II, George Stevens, William Wyler, John Huston, and Frank Capra were deeply affected by the years they spent in military service. So were James Stewart, Clark Gable, David Niven, and many other Hollywood people. Their experiences made them more serious, perhaps, about the issues facing mankind, and afterward they may even have approached their movie making, now and then, with more of a sense of mission. But the important thing was that they had new experiences which led them to new information about the world they lived in. Because they were better informed as citizens, they were better entertainers, too.

War may come again, and blast many people out of their accustomed rounds. But does it require a catastrophe to shake men free of their assumptions and jar them into the new experiences that lead to new awareness — and new usefulness? Individual men and women, understanding something of the roots of the communicative process, can plan new and vital experiences for themselves. Society will profit — indirectly, unpredictably, endlessly — from the information they carry back to work.

The flood of communication today is a towering, undefeatable fact. It is linked to the rising tide of economic well-being in the free countries — to the shorter hours of work and the resulting hours of leisure to spend. It is linked also to the rising tide of population, with its higher proportion of young people and old people who do not work at all. This vast empty reservoir of leisure is being matched by a flood of words and images — a glut of communication which can be in itself a destructive force.

Responsible selection is obviously a paramount social need. Faced with an overwhelming surplus, the consumer of communication cannot do all the deciding himself. As in politics the politician nominates and the people elect, so in communication, the writer or editor or producer nominates and the people make the final choice.

In the degree that the producer of communication is a man of conscience, he will select from the flood what is most valuable or most urgent. In the degree that he is an artist, he will cut through the flood of communication with a flair that will make his choices memorable.

The theatrical motion picture producer is only gradually becoming aware of his new position in the total framework of communication in America. It is a proud position, a position of considerable dignity and much responsibility. Freed somewhat from the studio bureaucracy, almost unrestricted by the Code, he has an audience as wide as the world. Forced to turn aside from assembly-line methods, he can now take the time to seek out those extraordinary stories which are worthy of a year or more of intensive creative work.

"I am looking," he says now, "for something special."

In that uncomfortable, indefinable phrase is summed up both the position and the problem of the Hollywood film maker today. His most desperate time of searching for subjects has come.

D. W. Griffith, the first great director of motion pictures, often quoted a line from a preface written by Joseph Conrad.* He quoted it so often that his forgetful idolaters have sometimes attributed it to Griffith alone. It is worth examining at somewhat greater length than the line he liked: "My task is, before all, to make you see." For what Conrad said of the writer of fiction the film maker must be willing to say of his own work as an artist:

. . . *if his conscience is clear, his answer to those who in the fullness of a wisdom which looks for immediate profit, demand specifically to be edified, counseled, amused; who demand to be promptly improved, or encouraged, or frightened, or shocked, or charmed, must run thus: My task which I am trying to achieve is, by the power of the written word to make you hear, to make you feel — it is, before all, to make you see. That — and no more, and it is everything. If I succeed, you shall find there according to your deserts: encouragement, consolation, fear, charm — all you demand — and, perhaps, also that glimpse of truth for which you have forgotten to ask.*

To snatch in a moment of courage, from the remorseless rush of time, a passing phase of life, is only the beginning

* For his novel, *The Nigger of the Narcissus.*

of the task. The task approached in tenderness and faith is to hold up unquestioningly, without choice and without fear, the rescued fragment before all eyes in the light of a sincere mood. It is to show its vibration, its color, its form; and through its movement, its form, and its color reveal the substance of its truth — disclose its inspiring secret: the stress and passion within the core of each convincing moment. In a single-minded attempt of that kind, if one be deserving and fortunate, one may perchance attain to such clearness of sincerity that at last the presented vision of regret or pity, of terror or mirth, shall awaken in the hearts of the beholders that feeling of unavoidable solidarity; of the solidarity in mysterious origin, in toil, in joy, in hope, in uncertain fate, which binds men to each other and all mankind to the visible world.

PART II

Hollywood at Work

INTRODUCTION

NOVELISTS and playwrights look for tension and violence when they hold the mirror up to the mirror of Hollywood. When Budd Schulberg analyzes *What Makes Sammy Run* or Clifford Odets examines *The Big Knife*, the necessity for dramatic conflict brings to the center of the stage a tough character vibrating with conceit or tyranny. Even when Hollywood holds up a mirror to its own mirror, there seem to be only three main stories to tell — the rising star, the faded star, and the vicious producer.

Newsmen, too, tend to seek out some kind of dramatic form when they write about Hollywood. They consider it their business to project its highs and lows, its glamorous days of triumph, its heartrending days of tragedy.

But there are other days in Hollywood. Every day is not clash and despair and compulsive villainy. There are thousands of hardworking hours when intelligent, experienced people, working together, manage to construct moments of artistry or fun through a combination of excitement and disciplined skill. Their story is a nonfiction story.

What I tried to do in my nine years of Hollywood reporting was to piece together a picture of Hollywood at work. My method was to seek out thoughtful people who were doing interesting things and ask them how they felt about the things they were doing. Usually we talked about the theme of the story or the cinematic ways to interpret the theme. I felt that my readers were interested in the film-making process and in those film makers who were serious about their work. Perhaps this was a "high-level" approach for so commercial a place as Hollywood. But it was the nonfiction way, the social scientist's way, if you will, and above all the way of a *Christian Science Monitor* man.

I must confess that I have, from time to time, looked forward to collecting some of my best "Hollywood Letters" in a book. The pieces I wrote at such times were usually terrible: the labor of trying to be significant shows its gritted teeth between the lines. The columns worth saving at all were often done in a hurry, with little thought of posterity or solemnity. From these, I have chosen a few that seemed to represent a variety of personalities and some of the continuing trends. Unfortunately some of the people I would most like to have included are not here. I hope these extracts from the *Christian Science Monitor*, 1951-60, at least reveal something of the flavor of the hardworking side of Hollywood during the decade of the television revolution.

The reader should remember the historical context in certain cases. Jimmy Dean was later killed in a highway crash; Hollywood has been trying, ever since, to find another actor like him. Nor is Dudley Nichols, Hollywood's most revered screenwriter, with us any longer. I have not tried to bring up to date the activities and films that came after my interviews, nor note the technical and economic factors which have changed. The film and TV combination known as Electronicam, for example, actually found few customers; a new kind of electronic camera, however, is beginning to be connected with both tape and film recording devices for certain TV shows. The Fox back lot, after many delays, was finally leveled, to be replaced by the planned real estate development. In 1962, Fox executives did make a hopeful announcement of a "new back lot" to be built near Malibu Beach, but it appears to be primarily a real estate investment. At about the same time, Revue Productions told stockholders that the big Universal-International back lot, acquired when Revue purchased the physical assets of the studio, would probably be disposed of, at least in part.

One of my sins of omission I can't fully explain, try as I may. It was my firm intention, when I began, to spend a lot of time with screenwriters. Something went wrong, and now I can scrape up only three relevant and valuable pieces — the one on Frank Gruber, the interview with Dudley Nichols, and one about Cary Grant, which attacks writers.

This is mostly my fault, but it also has something to do

with both journalism and the film medium. The best time to write a column about a single film, of course, is when it is in production. The producer, director, and stars are then available — but usually the writer is off the payroll and back home in Palm Springs or New York City. Furthermore, the producer is the one who actually decides whether to use the writer's suggested images and dialogue, and the director is the man who makes the film. If the reporter wants to know what's going to happen, he must talk to the people who make the final decisions.

The subordinate role of the writer in Hollywood is well known. There are a number of "hyphenated" men — writer-producers like Charles Brackett and Dore Schary, writer-directors like Billy Wilder and George Seaton. But when such men take on both jobs, it becomes still clearer that they are doing it because the decision-making job has the upper hand.

1

PRODUCERS

The Independence of David O. Selznick
January 21, 1958

"T O D A Y," David Selznick says, "the public goes in greater numbers than ever before to a few top pictures. The occasional film succeeds. The others don't.

"And so," he adds, with a massive shrug and a sweep of his hand, "if you don't succeed, you have a disaster. An independent producer and the people who put their faith in him simply can't get back their money after one big failure. You have to hit the center of the target every time.

"Yet in the nature of things, the independent way is the only right way to make pictures today. When I was at Paramount years ago we made fifty-two pictures a year and our executive judgments and prejudices and attitudes were imposed on every one of them. You can't make top pictures that way. You can only make assembly-line pictures. You can't make good pictures by a committee system, filtering them through the minds of half a dozen men. Besides, salaried people are not so likely to come up with big hits."

There is never any doubt about who is running the show during a Selznick picture. He has repeatedly compared a producer to the conductor of an orchestra — and the director to a mere concertmaster. On *A Farewell to Arms,* John Huston departed as director at an early stage and Charles Vidor took over. *Gone With the Wind* required the services of three different directors. It was made in accordance with the pre-production sketches Mr. Selznick supervised.

He was an independent of the present-day type even in the old days. Selznick International was an independent company releasing through M-G-M, according to much the same arrangement that nearly all pictures now made in Hollywood follow. The first version of *A Star Is Born, Nothing Sacred, Tom Sawyer, Rebecca,* and many other memorable films were produced by this arrangement.

His favorite films, incidentally, are *Viva Villa, David Copperfield, A Star Is Born, Rebecca* — "and of course *Gone With the Wind* must necessarily be included."

His opinions on the state of the business crackle with independence. Here are further points in his description of the way things are:

1. "This seems to be a poor period for the creation of great original work in any field of literature."

2. "It is increasingly necessary for movie producers to find original stories to produce, even though this does not seem to be the pattern right now. The best-sellers are priced out of all reason."

3. "If you are primarily concerned with something that is usually called personal artistic integrity, you don't belong in the business of making commercial pictures. You should get yourself a paintbrush or a typewriter."

4. "People who say the movies are going to come back to the position they had ten years ago are just ostriches. Television has killed the habit of motion picture attendance."

Sam Spiegel on the River Kwai
July 1, 1958

S A M   S P I E G E L was last heard from at the Brussels World Fair, where he told reporters he thought most Hollywood producers don't have any idea of the effect of their films overseas.

Where Mr. Spiegel will turn up next is anybody's guess. He is not as far-ranging or as much in the public eye as Mike Todd was. But he is one of the new breed of film makers who consider the whole world their stage. He is no longer a Hollywood producer. He has moved his residence to New York and makes his pictures as far away as possible from Southern California.

He comes by his globe-trotting naturally. Born and educated in Vienna, he first came to the U.S. in 1927 and was giving a series of lectures on European drama at the University of California extension in Berkeley when an M-G-M producer, Paul Bern, asked him to read and recommend foreign language stories for production. Soon after, he went to Universal Pictures and by 1930 was back in Europe at the Berlin office. When *All Quiet on the Western Front* arrived, to be made in European versions, he made it a personal crusade to show the film wherever he could in spite of official opposition, because he hoped its message might help avert war.

Following several independent productions in Berlin, Vienna, and London, Mr. Spiegel returned to Hollywood, was asked to produce *Tales of Manhattan,* joined with John Huston on *We Were Strangers,* and in 1950 reached his first great success with *The African Queen.*

Mr. Spiegel is unusual among movie makers: he is a reader and a man who respects intellect, a literate and highly complicated person, capable of alarming his more nervous show-business companions by falling into a deep and resolute silence. Where Mike Todd was an unpredictable force, Mr. Spiegel is an unpredictable focus of ideas.

With *The Bridge on the River Kwai* going into general neighborhood release in the cities and towns of America, its producer is telling even those moviegoers who go but twice a year: "This is the way things are." From the time two years ago when he bought the Pierre Boulle novel and a tentative script from Carl Foreman, he has been deciding what should be said to these millions of people.

Part of his message is that man is very largely an instrument of fatality. "Yes, it would be much more satisfying for you," he exclaims, referring to the most controversial scene in the picture, "to see Alex Guinness heading for

that plunger and consciously applying his hands to it —
deciding after all to blow up the bridge! But this would
be simply corny — like the Marines arriving at the last
moment.

"No. This is not possible for this man," he insists vehe-
mently. "He is the living proof that people basically
wish to build, not destroy, if left to their own devices. But
the very dilemma he faces at the end is the heart of modern tragedy and the secret of the emotional success of
the picture.

"He has wakened from his delusion that building the
bridge was what he most wanted to do. He says: 'What
have I done?' But he cannot bring himself to destroy the
bridge. When it is destroyed, it happens, like most things,
as much through fate as through decision.

"In fact the irony is that Jack Hawkins aims the mortar
at him and thus almost stops him from blowing up the
bridge. Every possible force prevents him from doing
the clear-cut thing!"

Mr. Spiegel, by his own admission, has read much in
Marx and Freud. Far apart as the poles in their purposes
and methods, these two influential writers do come together at a point which might be called materialistic de-
terminism. If this particular film producer believes that
societies and individuals are alike moved by vague pressures that predetermine individual decision, he is perhaps a reflection of certain predominant beliefs of his time,
as any producer must be.

In this particular case, however, Mr. Spiegel was not

himself forced by any vague pressures to go through the rationale described above. The original book simplified the whole thing by permitting the stubborn British colonel to thwart the British commandos entirely. The bridge is not blown up at all.

This outcome would not have carried such elaborate problems with it. But it would not have been very exciting, either. Therefore Mr. Spiegel, the maker of dramatic movies for a worldwide audience, laid down the law to himself. The bridge must go. It was a clear-cut decision, like the colonel's decision to build the bridge. It was neither vague nor subconscious, and it was his own. After that came the necessity for explanations.

Ross Hunter: Glamour First
August 18, 1959

ROSS HUNTER wants to go back to the tradition established by Louis B. Mayer. He wants to "put stars in cellophane wrappings."

In an era of "package deals" in Hollywood, Mr. Hunter appears to have a concept which outranks them all in box-office appeal. The premise is that people don't want to see "problems" on the screen — but they do like to cry a little. Entertainment, in other words, involves both laughter and tears. The important thing, according to Mr. Hunter, is to avoid the familiar realism which merely repeats the experience of the average moviegoer. The "problem," if there is one, must be heightened, "glamorized," placed out of context with everyday life.

"*Marty* was a very wonderful motion picture," he says, "but it never did make much money. Most people don't want to go see the very things they've been through, played out in rather humble, grim settings. They don't mind a familiar problem if it is lifted out of the familiar world and put somewhere where they can't quite touch it.

"I've been accused of making soap operas. That doesn't bother me at all. There's nothing wrong with soap opera if it's presented intelligently."

Mr. Hunter's way of presenting *Imitation of Life* resulted in the biggest grosses in recent history at Universal. Another remake, *Magnificent Obsession,* was also a surprise moneymaker. *All That Heaven Allows, Battle Hymn,* and *Tammy and the Bachelor* in succeeding years upheld his score. He has become known in Hollywood as a producer whose pictures appeal to women. "I've never had a flop," he says, "when I created a picture which had a glamorous image for the public. The stars like it, too."

Remakes, he claims, are more difficult to make the second time than the first. "You're living down a legend. Then, too, it has to be reworked to suit contemporary times. In *Magnificent Obsession* we threw out all but the last scene. In *Imitation of Life* the notion of inventing and manufacturing a pancake flour freeze didn't seem very exciting nowadays, so we placed the story in a theatrical framework instead."

For *Back Street,* the story of an unhappy marriage and

"another woman," the locale has been given an international flavor by shifting it to Rome. Instead of living in "a little hovel of a room in an attic," as Mr. Hunter expresses it, the woman is now a famous and very well-dressed designer, "with a right to make a name for herself." In the last scene she expects her lover to visit her for breakfast, but he is dying in an accident.

"I saw the old picture — the one with Irene Dunne — and I cried my eyes out! I like to make this kind of picture. I think there will always be a place for them. I don't want to hold up a mirror to life as it is. I just want to show the part which is attractive — not freckled faces and broken teeth but smooth faces and pearly white teeth."

The rising young producer was raised in an atmosphere of wealth, but he didn't gain success in Hollywood because he was related to anybody. He got "in" because he knew how to cut budgets.

Cleveland's Glenville High School remembers him as a good student who went on to Western Reserve University for a master's degree and came back to teach English and direct plays. His students sent a petition to the Paramount casting director, urging the studio to hire him as an actor. While their motives may have been mixed, their success was immediate. He was hired by Columbia and went on to make nineteen pictures.

After a year of illness, he was back teaching school again in Compton, California, where his students embarrassed him by recognizing him as "that good-looking guy in all those adventure pictures." Finally, Ann Sheridan helped him get a job as a dialogue director and later he got permission to "learn the business" (without pay) at one of the independent film lots. He watched camera-men, editors, sound men, and business managers. He learned how to get a lot of "production value" in a picture for small cost.

After a long campaign to reach the late Leonard Gold-stein on the telephone, young Mr. Hunter managed to convince that busy producer of cheap movies that he could help make them cheaper. He took $50,000 out of one budget by cutting down on the number of extras and by "changing two exteriors into one interior." That made him an associate producer, and after eleven pictures in eighteen months he was on his own.

It took him a while to persuade Universal that the audi-ence wanted *Magnificent Obsession* again. But he made it for $800,000, and the picture brought in $12,700,000. He still remembers those figures. That's one reason he's a fast-rising Hollywood producer.

Samuel Goldwyn on Leadership and Excitement
February 3 and 10, 1959

"Why don't they make good pictures more often?" For many people, moviegoers or not, this is the biggest ques-tion about Hollywood.

Perhaps the only adequate reply is another unanswera-ble question. Why aren't there more producers like Sam-uel Goldwyn?

Just as Cecil deMille's name was synonymous with grandeur and Louis B. Mayer was the apostle of family entertainment, so the Goldwyn label has always meant a relentless personal pursuit of quality. From story idea through casting to advertising, this is one producer who has always been insistently independent, meticulously determined to get things the way he wants them. He could wait for a year for Robert Sherwood to write *The Best Years of Our Lives*. He could wait through a dozen scripts for *Hans Christian Andersen*. When Sidney Poitier was "the right man" to play Porgy, he was sure he could win him over, even after he withdrew, at first, from the role.

Actually, Mr. Goldwyn says, it's impossible nowadays to "make good pictures more often." Fine stories and top talent are too rare and the audience too elusive. A producer should work on one picture at a time. When the Screen Producers Guild gave Mr. Goldwyn, a non-member, its annual Milestone Award, he read them the same lesson he has been preaching and practicing for many years: "We must concentrate on making fewer pictures.

"It is a startling fact," he pointed out, "that according to the published figures, although about 220 pictures were made last year, a mere 34 pictures produced practically one-half of the total domestic film rental received by Hollywood this past year.

"Study those figures — and study the pictures that produced those revenues — and then figure out for yourself if it pays Hollywood to keep on knocking itself out turning out pictures just to keep up with exhibitors' demands."

This doesn't mean that every "good" picture requires a top-heavy budget. Mr. Goldwyn had something else to say to the producers: "Conditions in the industry today are worse than I have ever known them in the 47 years I have been connected with motion pictures . . . I see people on all sides trying to outdo each other in demands that can ultimately mean only their own self-destruction and great harm to all of us."

In an interview a few days before the Screen Producers Guild dinner, I asked him whether he thought present conditions in Hollywood were due in part to the absence of responsible leadership.

"Oh, I've given up on that problem," he shrugged. "There never has been any leadership in this business."

I suggested that it was nevertheless true that he had frequently written national magazine articles, that he was looked on both here and abroad as a kind of spokesman of the industry.

"But I've always worked alone," he said. "I've never had a partner in 38 years. And anyway, this business is not like the steel business. Within the limits of the anti-trust laws, those steel fellows cooperate on standards of production and when one company leads, the rest follow.

"In Hollywood, everyone conducts his own business. Some of them are going out of business.

"We hold in our hands the well-being of this great industry which we all love, and it is up to all of us to come to our senses and face up to the facts of life — to live for the future, not in the past."

Mr. Goldwyn is living proof of the vitality of the way of life that looks to the future. After many popular and critical successes and the admiration of his peers, he is just as full of excitement about his current picture as he ever was about *Dodsworth, Whoopee, The Little Foxes, Pride of the Yankees, Wuthering Heights, Dead End, The Westerner, Stella Dallas, Arrowsmith, Our Very Own,* or *Guys and Dolls.*

"Any producer," he declares, "has to be excited about what he is doing, if he is worth his salt as a man and a creative worker. I make pictures to please myself. That has to come first — the personal excitement about a story.

"Of course you never succeed, even artistically, unless the public comes into the theaters to see the picture. And they won't come just because you've worked hard, or even because you've been excited. They only come in because there's something on the screen they want to see. The greatest spectacles are not crowds of people or big battle scenes, but whatever touches the hearts of the audience. When that happens, your excitement is worth seeing!

"We can't just depend on advertising and publicity. People ask me sometimes about the public relations of the movie industry. If we have good private relations and produce good pictures, our public relations will take care of themselves."

2

DIRECTORS

Delmer Daves' Route to the Top
March 11, 1958

"I NEVER laid a plan in my life," Delmar Daves insists.
Yet a motion picture director, of all people, has to be a
man with plans. A film is almost always shot without re-
gard to the order of the scenes in the script, and the
director is the one who must see that order at every moment. He has to be able to visualize every gesture and
movement, hear every word and sound, match in his
memory each "take" in the camera with the scenes that
belong before and after it. Mr. Daves himself expresses it
forcefully: "A director must have those cans of film all
stacked up in his mind before he ever starts shooting."

Perhaps he didn't precisely plan the moments which
advanced him from "prop man" through technical director to actor, writer, and director. But from the time he
decided on movie making instead of law, he knew he
wanted to be a director, and whatever he worked at on
the way, he did it indefatigably.

He started with a letter from a friend at Stanford who

was related to the production manager for James Cruze. He became a property man because he was willing to lift pianos if necessary. He followed the advice of an old hand and hustled so spectacularly that he could sometimes be seen in the day's rushes, dashing in front of the camera to arrange the scene for the next take. He attributes his earliest success to a day when he managed, with the help of a three-cent can of salmon, to get a cat to jump in the right direction.

Cruze took him to Metro with him and made him a technical director on a picture about college life. He became an actor unexpectedly when they needed "a big guy" for a villain. He became a writer in 1929 when Sam Wood discovered he had some ideas and asked him to write them down. He became a director in 1943 when he had done so much research on submarine warfare that nobody else knew enough to make his script for *Destination Tokyo* into a film.

Because he has been an actor — and primarily a movie actor — Delmer Daves knows a thing or two about the feelings of men and women who must face the cold eye of a camera. "A star is the loneliest person in the whole world," he says, "when he is alone in a close-up. When this time comes, I insist on the other actor in the scene reading his lines from behind the camera. That gives the one in the close-up the feeling that someone else is in the shot with him."

Mr. Daves is not an advocate, however, of letting actors do as they please. No one can be more caustic about the dangers of depending on inner feelings rather than over-all effect. He is not very happy about the times he has had to direct products of the Actors' Studio, for example. He has had to tell more than one New York performer, with all the force of his western personality, that the feeling of the actor is not the most important thing. "It's not up to you to feel it deeply," he says, "it's up to the audience. It's what happens to them that's important!"

Because his best-known film is one that broke new ground in the history of the western — *Broken Arrow* introduced the sympathetic Indian, Cochise — Mr. Daves is still known as a superior director of westerns. The most recent ones are *3:10 to Yuma, Cowboy,* and *The Hanging Tree.* But he is contemptuous of any notion that there is a separate "western formula." The test of a drama, for him, is "whether it could be set anywhere else in the world and still be a good story. The universal conflicts of good and evil are the dramatic elements that matter most."

Elia Kazan and the Veneer of Civilization
September 21, 1954

"I AM CONVINCED that movie audiences today are far ahead of the people who produce the pictures. They read a lot. Television has been expanding their horizons."

Elia Kazan is stretched out comfortably on a small divan in his small and rather uncomfortable office at Warner Brothers. He has just come in from his final sound-dubbing session on the film version of *East of Eden,* and he wants to relax. But his habits of alert observation and concentrated comment take no holiday.

"Picture executives have continually said to me: 'Oh, no, that is exactly what movie audiences don't want right now!' Then we finally go ahead and make the picture. And everybody wants it.

"Look how well *On the Waterfront* is doing. It has surprised everybody. And this is a pretty tough story, a painful story about a choice between good and evil. Nobody wanted it — except the audience.

"Mind you, I don't think what the audience wants is necessarily good. And I believe that a director, as an artist, can only make a movie the way he feels is right for him. But it's wonderful how people will so often stay away from the highly publicized pictures and discover those that are artistic and honest."

What about the criticisms of his last picture, especially those that call it "untrue" to the broader pattern of waterfront life?

"I was on the waterfront two years," he replies. "I lived with them. I know as much about the feel of it as any of the critics. These were men who knew that their fate was in the hands of other men. They were in a degraded position. This is the truth about them — I think the whole impression was exactly right. And what I was trying to make was not a piece of journalism or a documentary film but the story of this particular kid and what happened to the way he thinks.

"Violence? It's a brute fact of existence for them. It's part of their life. Their hero is always the tough guy. They don't fight all the time, of course, but the men they look up to are the ones they know are tough enough to win. You can't make a picture about them that doesn't take account of this.

"Do I have a preference for violence? No, and I don't think my record supports such a statement. Where is the violence in *Gentleman's Agreement* and *Pinky*? Or in *Tea and Sympathy*? I don't believe in violence for its own sake, or violence for purposes of showmanship. But when violence is an integral part of the story, there's no point in running away from it. Critics in the past have called me 'talky' almost as often as they said I like violence!

"It may be that we are so proud of our veneer of civilization that violence is more surprising and repugnant when it comes.

"*Waterfront* feels true to me — as *Streetcar* did. I like it the best of all my movies."

The man whom Brooks Atkinson once called "one of the most exciting actors in America" is still called "Gadge" by his friends because he is, as his Group Theater compatriots reckoned, a small, compact, and handy gadget to have around. Born in Constantinople, this bundle of energy was brought to America at the age of four. His father was a rug importer and nobody in his family ever had any previous connection with show business.

It was after Williams College, when he somewhat indecisively determined to prolong his education at the Yale Drama School, that he fastened on the objective of theatrical direction. Two years of hustling props and running errands for the Group brought him no pay but in time the title of "assistant stage manager." In 1935 Clifford Odets insisted on casting him as Agate in *Waiting for Lefty* and for six years he acted — including twelve weeks at Warner Brothers in Hollywood.

He finally got a directing assignment. *Café Crown* was only a mild success, but Thornton Wilder saw it and wanted him to do *The Skin of Our Teeth*, which won him the Critics' award. After that came *Harriet, Jacobowsky and the Colonel, All My Sons, A Streetcar Named Desire, Death of a Salesman*, and others. At thirty-four, he became a movie director, beginning with *A Tree Grows in Brooklyn* in 1944. He was also responsible for *Boomerang, Panic in the Streets, Sea of Grass*, the film version of *Streetcar*, and *Viva Zapata!*

East of Eden, which is based on the final chapter of the John Steinbeck best seller, he calls a kind of parable of Puritanism, a Cain and Abel story which tries to achieve modern understanding of the sources of evil. "I think most moviegoers realize," Mr. Kazan says, "that basically people are mixtures. They appreciate a film which shows that evil in human life may arise from good intentions — that evil sometimes comes, for example, from derailment of love."

The Notebooks of George Stevens
September 25, 1956

CAMERA work on *Giant* began May 18, 1955. Shooting (in Texas and Hollywood) was completed late in October. This is a long schedule, even for a picture intended to be more than three hours long.

But there were eight months of preparation before that. Once George Stevens, Henry Ginsburg, and Edna Ferber had decided to join forces to produce the film, Mr. Stevens had to prepare the script, select cast and crew, and decide on locations. Finally, after filming was completed, he had to put the picture together.

For Mr. Stevens, the editing process is the longest job of all. He has spent nearly a year on it.

William Hornbeck, his film editor, offers a quick summary of the Stevens approach to editing: "At first he'll try various things. He'll insert a close-up, shorten the scene. He'll go along that way — kind of half-heartedly fixing it up. Then all of a sudden he knows just what he wants. The result always seems simple and just right."

Of course a producer-director (acting as editor) can't "try various things" if he doesn't have enough film to do it with. Mr. Stevens, director of *A Place in the Sun* and *Shane* and a former cameraman himself, sees to it that William Mellor, his cinematographer, gets plenty of material from a variety of angles. For *Giant*, he took more than 400,000 feet of film.

He keeps an elaborate record on every "take." For *Giant,* there were fourteen thick volumes. Every strip of film, of whatever length, is catalogued by number and description, with an actual frame of film inserted on the page.

"We can't remember everything the camera gets," Mr. Hornbeck explains, "and sometimes after we have worked on a scene till it has become substantially different, we go back to the books and pick out a 'take' we had rejected before, because now it fits better with what we've got."

Several months ago, I spent a day at Warner Brothers just following Mr. Stevens around. I found him first in a tiny projection room, watching a scene which included Rock Hudson, Elizabeth Taylor, and the youngsters playing the roles of their children.

Suddenly the screen went black, and the actors started moving in reverse, talking gibberish. The projectionist had reversed the film and was taking the scene back to the beginning again. Some directors may want the light and sound turned off while it's being reversed, but Mr. Stevens is so aware of balance and tempo that he feels he learns something more about the scene even when it's going backward.

This particular set of shots went back and forth the same way, over and over, five, six — perhaps eight times. Every once in a while he and Mr. Hornbeck muttered something to each other. Mr. Stevens later told me they were working on the point of view.

"The shape of the scene as it stands," he explained, "is the children — and the audience — seeing the baby for the first time. But the emotion of the scene is the mother's response. We want to get into it more of the reaction of the mother. So we'll use another cut-in of her. They're cute children and the audience will respond to them anyway, but we aren't so interested in this feeling as we are in the personal one through identifying with her.

"These are small points, but they add up."

Later I followed Mr. Stevens into a room dominated by a console covered with dials. They were trying out the levels of sound for the big party scene just before Jett Rink gets his grimmest rebuff. We stood back of the panels to watch the ten-minute reel on the screen.

"A little more wind, I think," the producer-director said afterward. "There should be a real gust when he opens the door. And we'd better hold the music down a bit at the end, where Jett is left alone."

He added a few more technical suggestions — and explained the reasoning behind them as we walked over to the rehearsal stage to hear Dimitri Tiomkin conduct his new song for the picture.

"I want as much of a babble as possible in that party scene," he said. "It should be a little extreme, a little more than realistic. It won't hurt to hear them louder than they look."

William Wyler on Peace and Realism
June 26, 1956

"THE FRIENDLY PERSUASION," originally a series
of stories by Jessamyn West about a Quaker family and
their beliefs, has become a screenplay about the impact
of the Civil War on the eldest son.

William Wyler — producer-director of *The Friendly
Persuasion* for Allied Artists and Academy Award–winning director of *The Best Years of Our Lives* — has long
wanted to make this thoughtful, gentle, but controversial
film. "The picture may come as a surprise to many people," he suggests. "But I hope it will be a breath of fresh
air in an age of violence in entertainment.

"We aren't trying to 'sell' any particular approach to
war — the pacifist approach or any other. We simply
present a dilemma, a conflict between belief in country
and belief in a certain religious way of life. I do hope it
will be true, at least, that people who see this film will
think twice before they condemn all conscientious objec-
tors.

"We are not concerned in this picture with any 'collec-
tive' approach to peace, either. We are concerned with
the individual's feelings, and with the problem of following one's own conscience, even within a sect or group."

"Isn't this a 'problem picture,' then?" I asked.

"Not in the conventional sense — for two reasons.
First, we have tried to treat the story with a light touch.
We think this makes the point better anyway. In the sec-

171

ond place, the story happens in a period in the past. Therefore we are not preaching about problems of today, yet people will think about them all the same.

"Sometimes I wish we hadn't chosen to do a period piece," Mr. Wyler added, somewhat wearily. "It just doesn't seem to be possible nowadays to find an authentic location and point a movie camera at it without showing a lot of TV antennas or radio towers or neon signs. We traveled literally thousand of miles — Ted Haworth, the art director, and I — trying to find a farm area in Indiana or anywhere near there. We finally came right back here to the San Fernando valley and built what we needed. This was the only way we could accurately control the authenticity of the picture. And that's increasingly important. Moviegoers are more demanding than any other entertainment audience, and the hardest to please."

"Is that because the medium is more realistic than the stage?"

"Yes, that's part of it. I have filmed some plays" — among them are *Counsellor-at-law, Dead End, The Little Foxes, Detective Story* — "and I know certain effects achieved easily in the theater would be laughed off in a motion picture house. At a play, nobody cares whether the tree up there on the stage looks real or not. In a film, it's got to be perfect, or you get letters!

"But it's more than that. Mediocre work just doesn't pay off any more. The audience is much more critical than it used to be. The moviegoer is really more interested in people than in action."

"Would you call that a more difficult kind of authenticity?"

"I certainly would. It's not what is up there on the screen that is important, but what it makes you think or feel. You want to know what those people are feeling — you want to see behind their eyes."

3

WRITERS

Dissent by Dudley Nichols
July 29, 1952

DUDLEY NICHOLS views with alarm a trend which he feels has reached its peak — the dominance of the producer. Originally a man who watched over costs and mechanical details, the producer has become dictator of film content as well — the man really responsible for the whole operation.

"The director and the writer don't initiate pictures any more," Mr. Nichols declares. "In the old silent days, the directors made the pictures. If there was a scenario at all, it was just a guide. Even then, 'supervisors' were beginning to appear — men who saw to it that a certain number of films got made. This scheduling process grew stronger with the sound film. It was based on the necessity for filling theaters over and over again.

"Real estate investment made producers necessary. Those theater seats had to be kept warm. If great writers could not be found to turn out the needed footage, formula writers were brought in. A whole new class of people have come into the studios who do nothing but 'initiate properties' and say 'yes' and 'no' to proposed ways of handling them."

Mr. Nichols, who spent some of his happiest days working with director John Ford on *The Informer, The Plough and the Stars,* and *The Long Voyage Home,* evidently hopes that producers as a class may shortly go into decline. With the divorcement of theaters from production and the tendency of television to supply the public with "B" pictures, Hollywood may possibly be able to concentrate on fewer and better films. This has been proposed, predicted, and even promised by top executives.

Such a prospect draws a serene smile from Mr. Nichols, who looks forward with no alarm to (1) empty writers' stables at M-G-M and Fox, (2) cottages at Malibu filled with free-lancers planning to offer scripts to studios as they would offer books to publishers, (3) indigent producers pounding the pavements looking for work.

Writers have become producers. Mr. Nichols dissents somewhat from that trend, though he does not deny its importance. He has tried both producing and directing. He is convinced that either one "kills the writer in a man." The writer, he says, is functionally not a man of action; he is "necessarily introverted, living in the house of his own imagination."

Mr. Nichols wants to go back to the days when, he feels, picture making was more of an art — cooperative, to be sure, but dependent mainly on two joined forces, the director and the writer.

Frank Gruber's Seven Basic Western Plots
March 10, 1959

FRANK GRUBER has probably sold more western novels to Hollywood producers than any other contemporary writer. He is convinced that the western will be, for many years to come, a staple item both for theaters and for television.

"I can't explain the appeal the western has for Americans, beyond the fact that it's part of their own history and expresses a kind of basic morality. But the appeal is there. I started writing westerns — for money — a long time ago and I've never seen any reason for quitting."

Mr. Gruber is unimpressed by what are called "adult westerns." He sees them as nothing more than the same necessary stories with a few differences in characterization.

"After all," he insists, "there are only seven basic western plots. There's the cavalry and Indians story — haven't been many of them lately: they're due for a comeback. Then there's the 'Union Pacific' or pony express theme, where you are fighting the elements of nature to build a business or some other big project. These are usually big budget pictures.

"The homesteaders or squatters story, like *Shane,* for instance, has been a little overdone. Everybody knows about the conflict between the cattlemen and the farmers. But the dedicated lawman type is always good —

High Noon was like that, and many of the TV series: 'Gunsmoke,' my own show 'Wells Fargo,' and others.

"On the other hand, there's the outlaw story, humanizing or glorifying some outlaw like Billy the Kid or Jesse James. The revenge theme, with someone riding in pursuit of the man who wronged him, probably stems from the old *Riders of the Purple Sage.* The empire story, like *Duel in the Sun,* or *Broken Lance,* has the builder of a ranch or a way of life threatened with decline because of an outside threat or maybe a weak second generation."

Three elements have to be in every western, according to this practiced observer: a fistfight, some shooting, and some galloping horses. Without these, the viewer feels cheated; the writer omits them at his peril. In fact, the writer is pretty much obliged to set up a good fight in the very first reel, which in turn forecasts a much bigger (and usually more fatal) battle in the last reel. For a half-hour TV show, of course, more than one fight may not be necessary.

"There is always a big demand for television writers," Mr. Gruber claims. "But the producer of a series usually can't afford to take chances with unknowns. He wants writers who can solve their script problems the first time around. A very large proportion of the scripts we shoot are the first drafts the writers hand in. When we budget $1500 for a screenplay, we aren't eager to pay $432 more for a rewrite by another man.

"An action script shouldn't take too long to write. After we talk over the idea with the writer, we generally expect the completed job within seven days or at most two weeks. I've written many a teleplay in one day. Of course on our show we try to be, on the average, about ten weeks ahead of production, but some shows have to turn scripts over to directors within a few days after approval.

"How does an unknown become known? Well, that's pretty hard to say. Nobody will read your script if you just send it to them in the mail. They're too much afraid of plagiarism suits by authors who get their manuscripts back and then see a similar plot on the screen. So motion picture and television producers, as a general rule, send all thick envelopes back to the sender unopened. The writer has to have an agent. Then he'll send it to a producer and the producer will read it.

"It's not as hard, I think, to write for filmed television as it is to write short stories or novels. I consider myself primarily a novelist, but I write books with only Hollywood in mind. I started one novel some years ago that I wanted to finish, but somewhere along the way I realized it wouldn't make a picture, and I haven't finished it yet."

Cary Grant Is Dissatisfied with Writers
July 30, 1957

CARY GRANT occupies an almost legendary position in Hollywood. He is the first man everybody thinks of to play a leading role in a sophisticated comedy. But good sophisticated comedies are hard to find nowadays.

Mr. Grant has been shaking his head and making dissatisfied noises lately about the abilities, attitudes, and general public usefulness of screenwriters. "There used to be plays of wit and wisdom," he recalls, with that sad fall in his voice, "written by people who understood the meaning of words. Philip Barry and Frederick Lonsdale were like that — and Shaw, of course — men who polished their language, loved it.

"The modern idiom is getting worse," Mr. Grant continues, more sharply. "Writers seem to be less thoughtful. It's easier to write violent things. If you do flop, it's not so noticeable then, because some kind of audience will always respond to danger. If you kick them, they'll cry. But it's not so easy to make them laugh. It takes longer to write gracefully.

"Maybe the problem is that nobody is hungry any more. A writer can always get $1500 for a violence story on TV, so he doesn't take the trouble to do anything better. But what good is it when you have murder headlined all the time in the newspapers and that's all you get in the movies, too?

"If screenwriters do undertake comedy, they can only succeed, it seems, in turning out embittered comedy — the kind of thing in which everybody insults everyone else. It's really a great comedy, this business of living. Why can't movie writers write about it that way?"

There was a solemn pause at the end of this indictment. I was going to ask one of my favorite questions, but Mr. Grant proceeded to answer it first.

"Now, why do people laugh? Because what's happening on the screen isn't happening to them! But the adventure or joke or whatever it is must be plausible — it must have some recognizable truth in it, at least at first. What I try to do," he explains, cocking an analytical eyebrow, "is to take a man who is moderately bright, educated, and aware, and then put him in some kind of untenable position. Preferably it should be a position he gets himself into. The comedy comes from his attempts to extricate himself. Of course some elaboration around the edges is essential, and I like to work with a director who works such things out on the set as we go along. I often make suggestions for bits of business.

"But basically it's up to the writer. I never change anything blithely or thoughtlessly. If possible I try to find out from him why he wrote what he did. Sometimes a director says to an actor: 'If you don't like the scene, we'll cut it out.' That's a terrible thing. They should try to understand it — find out what is between the lines that the writer doesn't say and can't say in the limits of a screenplay. I found this to be of tremendous importance when I first knew Clifford Odets and I was working on *None But the Lonely Heart*. I thought the scene was all talk and wasn't getting anywhere. He told me: 'This man is too insecure to leave a silence.'"

Mr. Grant and I thought about that for a minute, and then I asked him what he had been reading lately.

"Oh, a wonderful thing on spiders. I'm fascinated by natural history and admire people who can concentrate on a fish or a leaf and know more about them than most of us can suspect about a human being. I'm beginning to realize, after many years of trying to fight my way toward success, how wonderfully rewarding it is just to examine everything around me. So often we are too busy to realize that we have never really seen a flower before. We should be able to listen — really listen — to what is going on around us."

4

STARS

Janet Leigh's Zest for Living
November 3, 1953

"I DON'T think you can ever stop learning." Janet Leigh is talking about what it takes to be a movie actress. She ought to know. She became one without any previous dramatic experience. She is as radiant and charming an example of a Hollywood "Cinderella girl" as you are likely to find.

"All my dramatic coaches have told me that I have an instinctive feeling of participation — this sort of thing!" She leans forward, her eyes alight with interest. Then she draws back, and adds: "But you must know exactly why you do everything. In *Prince Valiant,* for instance, I come rushing in to Bob Wagner's bedside after he has been wounded. I've got to know what has happened ever since the last time we met.

"The director, of course, is the one who helps you do that. He should tell each actor what the other characters are supposed to be thinking about. He should help you — but not too much!

"After all, you don't put on a part like a cloak." Miss Leigh is emphatic. "You don't lose yourself completely — you can't. And there must be some reason they assigned you to the part in the first place — something in yourself that they felt they had need of."

She frowns a little, afraid she is not being sufficiently modest, but rushes on. "People tell me often that I express a spirit of happiness. They do, really! And this makes me very glad. Because it means I have such a great opportunity to give!

"That means giving entertainment, of course, but maybe, once in a while, something more. Oh, I have fun playing a princess." She playfully strokes the long golden tresses provided by the Twentieth Century–Fox makeup department. "But if I can do something more difficult than that, it means a lot." Miss Leigh's eyes grow reflective. "If I can be just an ordinary kind of girl — a girl in a dime store — and still express a zest for living, a spirit of happiness —"

She nods and smiles, her eyes brighter than before (if that is possible). Then, satisfied that she is understood, she turns her attention to a steaming omelet.

It is easy to see why Norma Shearer was attracted by the picture of the receptionist's daughter at the Sugar Bowl Ski Lodge in Soda Springs, California — and why she persuaded M-G-M executives to bring young Jeannette Morrison to Hollywood. Not only did Miss Morrison become Miss Leigh, but she has also become Mrs.

Tony Curtis. She played her first film role in 1946. It will be a long time before she plays her last.

William Holden, World Traveler
March 23, 1954

"T h i s c a n b e an exhausting business," Bill Holden exclaims. "I've become convinced that there's no harder way of presenting drama than through motion pictures. On the one hand you may have to land with a helicopter on the deck of a ship just off the coast of Pusan. On the other hand you may have to spend hours going over and over an intense emotional conflict which leaves you limp as a rag.

"Last Saturday I spent the whole day yelling and screaming at Grace Kelly for that backstage dressing-room scene in *The Country Girl*. I was straining every nerve, just vibrating all day long, and when I got home I was so tired I couldn't move. It's a lot easier to jump on a horse, I can tell you!

"Harder than the stage? Sure, I think so," Mr. Holden insists. "I can never get excited about the strain the stage actor is supposed to be under. His three hours at the theater at least add up to a unified experience. He doesn't have to try and figure out what possible connectedness there can be between a scene shot two weeks ago ten thousand miles away and one that has to be finished up now on Stage 5."

Mr. Holden is very frequently ten thousand miles away. He'd like another chance to go to Europe soon. "Important things are happening there that are going to affect the balances of power in our time. I was in Italy during the last election, and it was frightening to see one hundred twenty-five thousand people cheering a Communist speaker in a Naples square.

"I wanted to do *The Bridges of Toko-Ri* especially because it might help meet a need for understanding in these days when America has bigger responsibilities overseas. On my trip to Korea for the Hollywood Coordinating Committee, I was supposed to ask the men what kind of entertainment they wanted. But one of the questions they most often asked me was what the people at home thought about the war. I couldn't find much to say. *Toko-Ri* tells the story of one young American who had to think through the meaning of Korea.

"Not that I'm a great one for message pictures!" Mr. Holden protests. "Along about the time I get too much of that kind of thing, I'll be off looking into the prospects for singing or tap-dancing lessons. Or asking for another picture like *Sabrina*. That was the biggest challenge I've had in a long time — to play the role of a completely irresponsible playboy. You'd be surprised how hard such a thing is for a man who was married at twenty-two and now has a responsibility to a family with three children. It went against all my instincts. I hardly knew how he would react to anything.

"It's getting clearer and clearer, though, that there is

a more educated audience for films. We can't go on making *The Knights of Arabia* over and over."

Marlon Brando on Achieving Understanding
October 19, 1954

THE SURPRISE about Marlon Brando is that, for all his carelessness, he frequently gives the fleeting impression of outdoing Rodin's "Thinker." He is a man who appears to live by the feelings of the moment, yet he obviously enjoys intellectual wrestling. He is not afraid to ask the meaning of a word. In a luncheon interview, he asked me what "microcosm" means — evidently someone told him *On the Waterfront* was one.

He will pursue a subject with a piercing, searching intensity and then switch it off almost casually. There is no denying the seriousness of the man on some subjects at some times, but he has no intention of getting serious enough long enough to be laughed at. He'll do the laughing himself, and do it first.

"An actor," he says sweepingly, "is at most a poet and at least an entertainer." Then he hesitates, half smiling. "I'd better stop and think," he remarks. "Do I really believe that?"

Evidently satisfied, he pursues the subject a little more. "You can't be a poet by trying real hard. It's like being charming. You can't become charming by working at it. But it is possible to try to live a creative and productive life. I feel," he complains suddenly, "as if I had eighteen granny knots in my neck. I hardly slept at all last night."

After a while, Mr. Brando can be persuaded to be thoughtful again. "Some parts are closer to you than others, of course, but they're all hard work. Sometimes you feel like being devoted to your job and other times you feel the antithesis. You aren't always walking with your head up into the sunlight, you know, feeling as if you have absolutely reached clarity and the elucidation of man's fate!

"Yes, I do feel a sense of growth as an actor over the last three years. But you probably think I'm more idealistic than I am about my job. I didn't especially choose acting. I just decided to take a whack at it. Kazan and I only work for ourselves, not for any big, vague idea of the cinema art. We just happen to manage to give each other something in exchange, that's all.

"That picture was the worst ever for physical considerations. Man, it was cold, I tell you! Some days the 'blood' froze on my face."

What about the influence of a performance on audiences? What about the deeper meaning for society, in other words, of the job he is doing?

"Well, I don't know. I suppose that's like the old Indian proverb about the leaf and the tree—'not a leaf moves that the tree does not know.' Maybe a film does have an influence on people's lives. But I don't think there's really any way to impart experience. And it's only through experiencing something that you're aware of the value of it.

"The hard thing is to get understanding. A wise man might be able to put his whole philosophy in one paragraph, but the hard thing is to understand what he means. I think when people look at a movie screen they pull the grid of their own frame of reference over it. They only correlate what happens on the screen with their own experience."

Didn't *A Streetcar Named Desire* provide a pretty shattering experience for the audience? "Well, I guess you can articulate experience, but you can't really share it. Maybe *Streetcar* got over some understanding of other peoples' difficulties. It didn't offer much hope but there was a kind of hope born out of recognition."

James Dean and the High School Kids
July 12, 1955

THERE SEEM to be a good many versions of James Dean's approach to life, and it may well be that most of them are founded, more or less, on fact. Newcomers in Hollywood are likely to be misinterpreted, in any case. Some of them encourage conflicts in interpretation: such conflicts are dramatic and likely to focus attention on the subject.

I can report on only one or two aspects of this controversial young man, based on a single encounter on the set. I got an impression of powerful "intensity" (so necessary for survival in show business) and of keen intelligence.

In *East of Eden,* his first Hollywood appearance, he played the starring role of a son who insisted he was not loved. As a kind of archetype of whining delinquents — the Cain of the undisguised parable in the picture — he was far from an appealing figure. Nevertheless, countless feminine moviegoers of all ages evidently watched his shambling gait and listened to his inarticulate yearnings with maternal devotion. John Steinbeck's "misunderstood" juvenile character of 1914 found sweethearts and mothers aplenty in 1955. Many of them wrote letters — the kind of fan mail that has ranked him with the top four or five actors in popularity.

Jimmy Dean doesn't necessarily shamble or mumble. He knows a thing or two about the rising generation, and has discovered that most of them do not stand like ramrods or talk like Demosthenes; therefore, when he plays such roles he tries to imitate life. It is the romanticized conception of the juvenile, he declares, in round, clear tones, "that causes much of our trouble with delinquency nowadays. *The Wild One,* for instance — it had, so far as I can see, no good effect. It just encouraged these kids to go out and buy black leather jackets and a motorcycle and act like Brando in the picture.

"This picture?" The new bobby-sox idol, star of *Rebel Without a Cause,* leans on a nearby floodlight with one hand, adjusts his horn-rimmed glasses with the other, and stares somberly at the floor, framing his words. "I think one thing this picture shows that's new is the psychological disproportion of the kids' demands on the par-

ents. Parents are often at fault, but the kids have some
work to do, too.

"But you can't show them some far-off idyllic conception of behavior if you want the kids to come and see the
picture. You've got to show what it's really like, and try
and reach them on their own grounds.

"You know, a lot of times an older boy, one of the fellows the young ones idolized, can go back to the high
school kids and tell them, 'Look what happened to me!
Why be a punk and get in trouble with the law? Why
do these senseless things just for a thrill?' I hope this film
will do something like that. I hope it will remind them
that other people have feelings. Perhaps they will say,
'What do we need all that for?'

"If a picture is psychologically motivated, if there is
truth in the relationships in it, then I think that picture
will do good."

Joanne Woodward Works from the Outside In
November 11, 1958

JOANNE WOODWARD, who won her Academy
Award for playing a woman with three different personalities in *Three Faces of Eve*, is properly contemptuous of
easy definitions, categories, labels. She pretends, with
a deprecatory shrug, that she is actually quite faceless —
"the real me is all the parts I've played!"

The real Joanne Woodward is more than that — and
a good deal more than Hollywood is used to. She is clear-

headed, confident, and exceptionally frank. She comes from a well-to-do Southern family and reads books. There is nothing fluttery or fuzzy about her. She has a rare kind of authority, on or off the screen.

She thinks suddenly of a story about herself. "I waved hello to Marty Ritt the other day — like this." She twirls her wrist in a languid, graceful gesture. "He came over to me. He asked me, 'Was that really you that waved just now?'

"I laughed and said, 'Of course! I'm all dressed up. I'm a lady now!'

"I play whatever I'm wearing. Ever since I was a child, that's been true. I was always a great one for dressing up. I always knew I was going to be an actress, of course. There was never any doubt of that. I never thought about being a movie star, particularly. I wonder what it is like, being a star? It must be dreadful. And how do you know you really are a star?

"I've never been able to understand why an actor just wants to play himself. I'm a character actor — I like to change myself into something else — put on makeup and wigs and things. I think I play best the parts that are far away from myself. Quentin, in *The Sound and the Fury*, is closer to me than most, and she was hard to feel sure about. Marty said one thing that helped — and I think it was practically the only thing he did say. He said: 'She has a tremendous appetite for any experience. When she cries she really cries. When she laughs she really laughs. There's no halfway measure for her.'

"But I didn't really find the character until I had my hair cut. After that, I knew just what to do.

"*Three Faces of Eve?* Yes, that was different — more of an inner thing, because often the transitions had to come when I was in the same clothes. I just had to take a deep breath, press a button, and assume the other personality."

For a woman of such ready wit and keen intelligence, Miss Woodward is curiously reluctant to analyze her art. "I think the worst thing for me to do would be to intellectualize my relationship to a part. I don't like to talk to anybody about a role before the picture begins, or while it is shooting. I don't think it should even be necessary to talk very much with the director. He should leave you alone as much as possible.

"I find myself quite inarticulate when I talk about a character. For me, acting has very little to do with the intellectual process as such. Some of the groundwork may be intellectual, perhaps. But the only general rule you can make is that whatever works for you is right for you.

"Some people work out from the inside. For me, things like costume and hairdo are quite important. I work from the outside in.

"Laurence Olivier, you know, tries things in front of a mirror. But that didn't work for me. I tried it once, and the only thing that happened was that I broke up. I just couldn't stop laughing at myself."

Judy Holliday Analyzes Comedy
August 10, 1954 and April 24, 1956

"IT'S AN ephemeral thing," she says, with a keen, far-away look. "All I know about comedy is that it's hard — very hard. Suddenly where there was something, there's nothing. So often that happens!

"Oh, I have some theories, all right." Judy Holliday shrugs and smiles that sweet, expansive smile which always contrasts so unexpectedly with her usual air of repressed mischief. "But every time I'm tempted to develop the subject it turns out to be a mistake. Theories always come after the fact, and when another fact comes along you have to develop a new theory. I hate being glued to one theory — it's a trap, even if it's one I make myself."

Anybody meeting and talking with Miss Holliday for the first time almost always has to go through a curious process of shifting gears, conversationally speaking. You may have heard frequently enough that she is intelligent and thoughtful, yet her role as the damsel with the scattered brain is much too familiar and persuasive to be put aside easily. And her tone of voice is practically the same, off screen or on. "I seem to be blessed," she points out plaintively, "with fine pumice somewhere around my vocal cords."

But the more you talk the more you realize how careful she is about what she says. She thinks ahead about it, takes time to choose. This is a deeper thoughtfulness than her easy familiarity with ten-dollar words like "ephemeral."

"Oh, yes, there are certain staple items in comedy," she says, "like the falling-down bit, or the surprise buildup with the thing that happens twice and then is different the third time. You can predict laughter to a certain extent.

"But I'm absolutely certain that being a good actor or comedian has nothing to do with intelligence. I've seen people with no horizons whatever who have perfect timing on the stage. Of course intelligence doesn't necessarily hold you back. I'm sure it helps in getting better material.

"Sometimes when I'm trying to do a scene I get terribly aware of myself. I see myself doing it. That's no good. It's like self-sabotage. George Cukor used to get blue with fury when I'd do that. He should. A director has to shake you out of it. It's all right to think about how your face looks when you're doing an imitation. But in a regular dramatic or comedy scene, if you do that, you're finished.

"Comedy," she frowned, "has to be believable. But it can't be too real — you know what I mean? It's a delicate difference. Some of the fight scenes between Jack Lemmon and me in *Phffft* had to be cut — they were too realistic to be funny. Yet there are scenes in *The Solid Gold Cadillac* where I threw away laughs right and left, because we wanted to keep a sense of believability.

"I remember one line that we wanted to make funny and weren't sure how to do it. The chairman asks if there are any questions, and I get up and say, 'Yes, I have one — I understand the chairman earns $175,000 a year.' He says, 'What is your question?' And I say, 'My question is why?'

"Now what is the funniest way to say that? Should I pause just before the word 'why'? Should I say it with a kind of shrug? Should I give it the exact inflection the chairman gives his question? Or should I say it all at once on one flat level — my-question-is-why? You tell me after you see the picture whether it gets a big laugh.

"I don't mind saying," Miss Holliday concluded, "that before I got into this business myself I used to have a kind of intellectual contempt for comics and for all the silly Babbitts in the audience who wanted to laugh at jokes. But when I grew up and began to find out there were troubles in the world, I wanted to laugh myself — and found it hard.

"Then when I started to make other people laugh, I found my greatest reward was to get letters from people who were depressed or ill or unhappy or shut-in. They were so grateful to be able to laugh and forget for two hours! Believe me, I was never again scornful about comedy or about the people who need it."

Alec Guinness Wins His First Laugh
February 7, 1956

THERE WAS one special question I had long wanted to ask Alec Guinness should he ever come within asking distance: what is it that makes people laugh?

Like most skilled comedy stars, he at first replied, "I just don't know." Then he went on to tell me a story about the first laugh he ever extracted from an audience.

"When I was twenty-one," he said, "I was an understudy in a London show. It was full of stars — Edith Evans, and so on. After a while I was promoted to a better part, in which I actually spoke two or three lines. I had to cross the stage with an armload of baggage, put it down, and then put a question to somebody who was standing there.

"Now the man I replaced always got a big laugh from the audience when he asked that question. I knew I could get a much bigger laugh. I'd have sworn I was a better actor than he was. So I went on that first time, bursting with confidence, and didn't get any response at all. Not a titter!

"The cast, of course, was used to hearing a laugh at that point. They must have been as much surprised as I was. But nobody said anything.

"I began to wonder how I should revalue the situation. My entrance became just a little bit more desperately different each night. Still — nothing. Finally Edith Evans took pity on me. She was very grand, you know, and didn't speak much. She was waiting there in the wings as I came off, because she went on shortly afterward.

"'You know what's wrong, don't you?' she said to me quite suddenly on the fourth night. 'You really ought to get that laugh. You're twice as good an actor as that other man. But you're alienating the audience. You go on that stage with a knowing look in your eye, practically proclaiming that you want them to laugh.'

"I knew it was true. I was pressing it too much — pushing it. What I said should seem unexpected. The following night, I knew what to do. I couldn't possibly describe what it was, then or now. But I got a tremendous roar from the audience. It was much bigger than the other fellow got! I was very pleased with myself.

"The very next night — nothing. I was completely at sea. I thought I'd got it and then I didn't have it at all.

"But she said that was all right. 'No, you won't be able to do it for about a week now,' she told me. 'You will have to learn how you did it correctly the first time — and relax with it. Then you'll have it.' And it worked exactly that way.

"So you see, it is very hard indeed to explain what comedy is. It can be very subtle and tiny and minute. Fashions change, too. Everybody shudders nowadays when you mention satire, and they say it never pays at the box office. It's difficult to bring off, yet for that very reason it may be the most appealing from the performer's point of view. I think probably *The Man in the White*

Suit is my favorite among the comedies I've done. It's certainly in the category of satire.

"I suppose really," he added, making at last an oblique attempt to answer my question, "comedy depends upon the unexpected. There is the opposite rule, too, that the audience loves to know ahead of time what is going to happen to some unsuspecting person — a surprise behind a door, for example. There you have actually the repetition of the expected. But the next time around perhaps the thing isn't there at all, and the audience is even more delighted.

"It may be nothing more than an unexpected expression on someone's face, but when something different happens" — he snapped his fingers sharply — "there you have it. They laugh!"

5

THE CHANGING SCENE

Raymond Hatton Remembers the Silent Days
April 29, 1958

"THOSE WERE the days when everybody was in there punching."

Raymond Hatton is thinking back to his memories of the silent film days. "You felt as if you were an important part of what was going on. If you didn't get down to the studio at nine o'clock, you felt sure the studio would collapse."

He smiles and shakes his head. "That had its practical aspects, too, in those early days of small companies. When I was working for the Christy Brothers — that was right near Gower and Sunset Boulevard in Hollywood — you remember, they used to call it Gower Gulch because they made so many westerns there. Well, when I worked for the Christy people, there was a bank at the corner of Hollywood Boulevard and Cahuenga, just a couple of orange groves away. And when we fellows got our pay checks, we used to get over to that bank just as fast as we could before the company's money was all gone!"

Mr. Hatton is now working from time to time in television — a business which has its similarities to the hectic days of silent films, but has already passed its pioneer era of fast-multiplying fly-by-night companies. Recently he played an old prospector in an episode of "Death Valley Days," but he seems especially happy talking about the old days.

"You know, I didn't know what this movie business was at first. Somebody told me there was this company shooting films over in Glendale one morning, and I was out of a job so I went over to see. I still felt as if I wanted to hear them rattle those programs out front, and hear those seats flop down when people came into the theater before the curtain goes up. But I was willing to try anything once.

"Well, I stayed on. I was with Biograph when Mack Sennett was there, and Mary Pickford and Mabel Normand. And when Sennett set up the Keystone company, I went along and was with them two years. I was one of the few in that outfit who never played one of the Keystone Kops — and I never fell in the mortar box either!

"I was with the Jesse Lasky company and with Paramount for fourteen years, when Wally Reid and Dusty Farnum were there. It was all on open stages, you know, since it was silent. And the only lighting controls we had were the 'diffusers' — spread out on wires that ran the length of the stage — to keep the sunlight out when we wanted that.

"I remember *Joan the Woman* with Geraldine Farrar and the back-lot battle at Universal City when the cameramen worked in the trenches — eight or ten of them. It was the first time deMille used his telephone system. He'd tell them when to start grinding on number two and number three — that kind of thing."

Mr. Hatton says he used to like to go into movie theaters and watch the audience, especially to see how one of his running gags was working out. He remembers one time going into a little film house on Hollywood Boulevard, now no longer in existence. He sat behind a young fellow who was really caught up in the action, and was talking to himself about it.

"Boy," he muttered happily to himself as he watched Mr. Hatton approach the unhappy villain near the end of the comedy reel — "Boy, you're gonna get it! You're sure gonna get it!"

Then, after the inevitable kick that sent the bad man sprawling, and while the uproarious laughter in the movie house was dying down, Mr. Hatton heard him whisper while he was still gasping for breath: "I told you, boy! I told you you was gonna get it!"

That one, Mr. Hatton reflected with fond satisfaction, worked.

Hannibal's Elephants in Southern California
September 7, 1954

"I won't go back to Carthage till I batter in the gates of Rome!" So speaks the modern musical Metro version of Robert Sherwood's comedy hero, Hannibal.

In *Jupiter's Darling* (which still bears some resemblance to *The Road to Rome*) it is Esther Williams who interferes with Hannibal's plans to batter down those gates. As Amytis, the bored betrothed of the Roman dictator, Fabius Maximus, she slips across the lines to get a look at the famous Superman, falls in love with him while helping him swim a river, and finally permits herself to be taken away in exchange for the city of Rome.

Historians may blanch at these liberties, but M-G-M authorities on entertainment retort that no historian has been able to think of anything better to explain Hannibal's withdrawal. There is no particular reason, they say, why the story couldn't involve not only a beautiful woman, but also some swimming and singing.

Why not, too, have Marge and Gower Champion as a couple of dancing slaves who fall in love with each other? And with their unexcelled gracefulness available, why not contrast it with the swaying hulks of some of those elephants Hannibal had around?

All this, and more, is accomplished by George Wells, George Sidney, and Dorothy Kingsley, who are respectively producer, director, and writer of this lavish extravaganza. In the course of elaborating on the mysteries of a more or less historical event, they have used eighty-two sets. Miss Williams wears more than twenty-five outfits designed by Helen Rose. Howard Keel (who else could be a musical Hannibal?) appears in twenty different suits of armor, leather, and fur, designed by Walter Plunkett.

Mr. Keel was lolling atop the leading elephant the day

they had the biggest show. On six hundred acres leased for location work in the mountains northwest of Los Angeles, the CinemaScope cameras, wide-ranging as they are, were having a hard time taking in everything that was going on.

There were ten elephants with foot-long spikes on their foreheads and comfortably shaded riders on their backs. There were four hundred fifty extras clothed in all colors of the rainbow (including chartreuse), carrying purple banners and making a great noise. The noise turned out to be a song, much more understandable when the pre-recording was turned on over loudspeakers: "Hannibal, oh Hannibal! We love to fight for Hannibal — the high and mighty Hannibal!"

There were other items not picked up by the Cinema-Scope cameras that day. For one thing, among the crowd of extras there were eight assistant directors, dressed like Hannibal's warriors, but carrying concealed walkie-talkie radios for communication with Mr. Sidney. The elephants' trainers, too, wore costumes.

The cameras kept no record of several rehearsals when the elephants were required to amble purposefully along in the general direction of Rome — and then come back around past the mess tent and the parked automobiles and the assembled kibitzers to do it all over again. And when the cameras finally started turning, there was no record made of Mr. Sidney's shouted reminder: "Take off your glasses and wristwatches! Somebody move that MG — it's in the picture!"

TV Tools for Hollywood?
October 9, 1956 and September 30, 1958

ELECTRONICAM is a superduper double-duty thing-amajig which rents for $750 a week at the very least. It combines a regular old-line Mitchell film camera with a live television camera. At that price, you'll have to bring your own Mitchell, but the management will supply TV viewers and a couple of trailers full of equipment.

The idea is for the director to forsake his fabled canvas-back chair (usually planted among the lights, props, and other paraphernalia), and look at a tiny screen, not the action itself. He can watch exactly what is going onto the film at the very moment it is being recorded. He is to be a TV and film director at the same time, and if he's the speedy type, he can edit the film by means of his cut-ins from two or three different cameras. If electronic tape ever replaces film, he can use that, too.

In an all-week series of showings, the DuMont Laboratories demonstrated to guild and union members, executives, press, and other glumly interested onlookers how easy it is to put off the old methods and put on the new. Blithely the young men sat astride the newfangled equipment and steered it back and forth across the floor, while a shirtsleeved young director whispered terse instructions over the intercom. Here was TV production with a vengeance — fast, furious, exacting.

"They'll never get me to do that," muttered many a

veteran of meticulous motion picture photography. "Anyway, you can't get the lighting right when you're in such a hurry. And to accommodate more than one camera you have to compromise and use full, flat lighting. You can't make quality pictures that way — the kind of pictures the public expects from Hollywood."

Altogether, it was not a comfortable confrontation, this meeting of old and new. The show was indirectly sponsored by Paramount Pictures. It took place on the very sound stage (formerly Warners) where Al Jolson put on wax the historic words and music that started off the era of sound. It took place against a background of movie-TV mixup few veterans would have predicted even two years ago. As they sat watching the new gadgetry — which incidentally was recording a maudlin story of murder and marital infidelity — the background of change was very much on their minds.

On top of everything else, Hollywood is facing the videotape era.

Up to now, film making has involved both physics and chemistry. Optical principles governed the work of the cameraman. He had to think in terms of amounts of light and distances from the lens. Then, when that rectangle of light hit the film at the back of the camera, something happened to the exposed emulsion which a technician at a laboratory had to bring out by passing it through tanks full of chemicals — first for the negative, later for the positive print.

All this took a number of hours — and still does for

theatrical pictures and most TV dramas. The director doesn't actually know what he has on film until the next day when he sees the "rushes." Not until after the whole film is shot does he usually go to work with the editor and put the picture together.

With electronic tape, the show can be run off again within a few seconds after it is shot. The director can see at once what the whole performance looks like; he can do it over again if he likes, or some part of it. The technical work is all done with electronics. No chemistry at all. No laboratory. But this also means that the plain brown tape can't be read without a machine to read it, and a very complicated, expensive machine it is. Videotape editing is still in the experimental stage, but TV people insist "they'll lick this problem" eventually.

A whole way of life is wrapped up in the spool of film that goes into the camera, "rolls" during shooting, is processed at the lab, gets cut up by the editor, goes back to the lab for final printing, and finally unwinds in the theater projection booth — or on television. Theatrical films will be made on the old-fashioned strips of acetate for a long time to come. Only chemistry can provide the exacting quality needed for the wide screen. But tape might have a more fundamental effect on Hollywood's way of life than the picture tube in the parlor, which started all the trouble in the first place.

The Vanishing Back Lot
April 22, 1958

OUT ON the back lot at Twentieth Century–Fox, exposed to wind and weather, lined up quite formally in two facing rows, are about twenty or thirty different kinds of stairways. They reach up from the ground, some straightforward and wooden, some appearing to be made of stone, others curving in steel serpentine, stretching up and probing out into space in every direction.

There is always something eerie about a major studio back lot, even in the bright light of midafternoon. There is a sense of the past hovering over abandoned streets, long empty of the horses' hoofs which thundered to box-office success on the screens of the world. There is a feeling of fantastic make-believe about the fronts of the buildings on "the New York street" or "the Boston street," solemnly backed by nothing but wooden slats.

But there is also the ever present pattern of potentiality. The empty villages — the huge blue sky-drops — the empty cement reservoir — any of these may come to life tomorrow to be used again in a motion picture. Workmen will turn up early in the morning to refurbish and repaint, change the signs and shift the turf. And on the day after, cameras and actors will move in.

This will not happen much longer on the back lot at Twentieth Century–Fox. Soon workmen will start to clear the area of all its motion picture trappings and prepare it to become a big new real estate development in West Los Angeles, dotted with enormous apartment houses and perhaps, if all goes well, a movie theater.

Here is the street where they did the exteriors for *A Bell for Adano*. There is the Boston street where *The Man in the Gray Flannel Suit* walked. Not far away is an old log fort which once protected Shirley Temple, and the grotto used for *The Song of Bernadette*. The stocky columns used first for *The Egyptian* are still painted as they were redone for *The King and I*. The Southern mansion, the picturesque French village with the bridge over the little empty cement "river," the enormous castle partly burned down for *Prince Valiant*, the jungle area, the lake, the lane of pine trees, the elaborate garden with its innumerable kinds of flowers and plants — all must go, even the western street. If you turn the right corner, you can find a copy of Grauman's Chinese theater, its box office put aside, windowless and dejected.

Today the audience is more fickle than ever. Every motion picture studio is staring down from dizzy budgets into a smoggy void of doubt. It is hard not to look at the passing of the Fox back lot, as a local newspaper headlined a picture story about it, "Last Look at a Make-Believe World: Doomed by Progress." What is it that is doomed? The back lot? Or a whole era of the wonderful make-believe world that is the movies?

The past weighs heavily on the Fox back lot this spring, although it is the newest back lot in the industry. Show business would not be the same without this sense of nostalgia. But its characteristic cry is, "Leap before you look!" And for many daring divers who are fortified with talent and a sense of timing, the leap into the unguaranteed future is still exciting and enormously rewarding.

Those twenty or thirty indeterminate groping stairways symbolize the very nature of show business — that "stairway to the stars" which every film producer blithely mounts, over and over again, in the hope that there will be a solid audience waiting at the top.

79480